IP-13   2x10(07)

The
Mouse

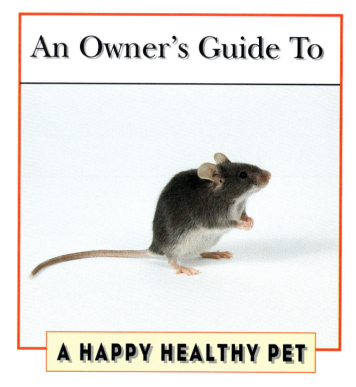

An Owner's Guide To

A HAPPY HEALTHY PET

Howell Book House

Hungry Minds, Inc.
Best-Selling Books • Digital Downloads • e-Books • Answer Networks
e-Newsletters • Branded Web Sites • e-Learning
New York, NY • Cleveland, OH • Indianapolis, IN

Howell Book House
Hungry Minds, Inc.
909 Third Avenue
New York, NY 10022
www.hungryminds.com

For general information on Hungry Minds books in the U.S., please call our
Consumer Customer Service department at 800-762-2974. In Canada, please
call (800) 667-1115. For reseller information, including discounts and premium
sales, please call our Reseller Customer Service department at 800-434-3422.

Library of Congress Cataloging-in-Publication Data
Shulman, Stephanie.
The mouse : an owner's guide to a happy healthy pet / [Stephanie Shulman].
    p. cm.
Includes bibliographical references.

ISBN 1-58245-006-4

1. Mice as pets.   I. Title
SF459.M5S54   1999
636.9'353—dc21   99-37567
                          CIP
Manufactured in the United States of America
10 9 8 7 6 5 4 3 2

Series Director: Kira Sexton
Book Design: Michele Laseau
Cover Design: Iris Jeromnimon
Illustration: Laura Robbins
Photography: All photographs by Eric Ilasenko unless otherwise noted.
Production Team: Hungry Minds Indianapolis Composition Services

Contents

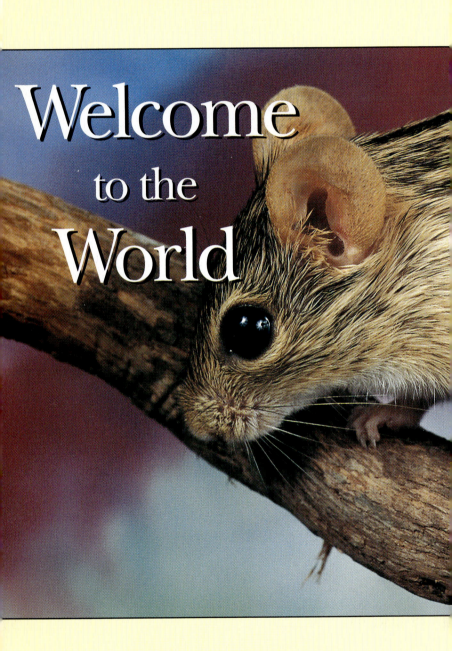

Welcome
to the
World

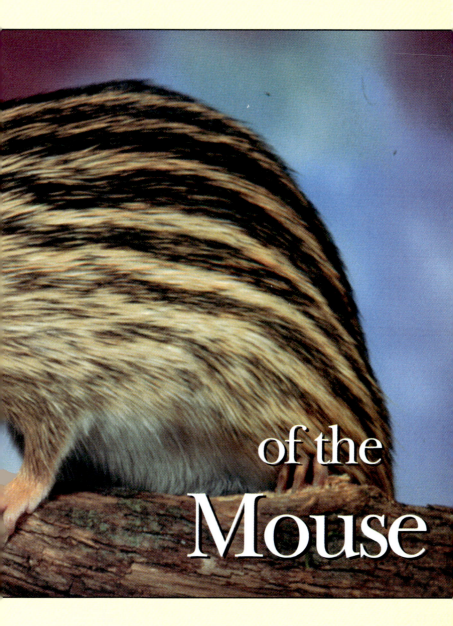

of the
Mouse

External Features of the Mouse

Whiskers

Nose

Mouth

Eye

Ears

Paw

Back

Underbelly

Base of Tail

Tail

chapter 1

The History
of the
Mouse

How could anyone not love sweet and gentle mice? If you were to hold mice and study them for even a brief period of time, you would soon recognize their spectacular nature. Mice have perfectly engineered bodies and are able to move with the greatest agility. Their constant curiosity excites them into action. Their lovable faces peer at you  inquisitively, and their tiny paws grasp firmly as they climb into your pockets, looking for a special treat.

Based on their friendly nature alone, mice are marvelous pets for people of almost any age. Through years of breeding, their skittish nature has been refined to reveal a tamer animal that enjoys human companionship.

Some people do not consider the mouse to be a proper pet. These people regard the mouse as a pest that destroys property and carries disease. Even though we now understand the joy that smaller creatures can bring to us, the mouse is still one of the most misunderstood of pets. Many people do not see the benefits of having such a small friend. But the mouse is an active and social creature.

MAN VERSUS MOUSE

Mice are believed to have evolved in Asia about 40 million years ago, during the Eocene epoch of the Tertiary Period of the Cenozoic Era, at least 3.8 million years before the appearance of modern man!

These pocket pets, as they are sometimes called, love to explore and interact with you. They are fastidious animals, constantly grooming themselves, washing their fur, cleaning behind the ears with their paws and tidying their tails. These curious creatures are always ready to investigate. Mice become tame and make great friends. Man's ongoing relationship with the mouse has benefited us in research and education as well as in friendship and fun.

If you are thinking of getting a mouse, you must ask yourself: Am I ready to become an active participant in my new pet's life? You must have the time to provide not only food, water and housing, but also quality friendship. Creating and maintaining a bond with this little creature provides you with hours of fun and valuable insight into the animal kingdom. In return, you become your pet's voice to the human world. You keep him safe and warm, providing him with playtime and—if necessary—medical attention. If you feel you have even thirty minutes a day to devote exclusively to this pet, you are ready for a mouse.

The Adaptable Mouse

Mice do well wherever they go. They are highly adaptable creatures and live well in varied conditions. They are omnivores, which means they eat both plants and animals. Indeed, mice are willing to make a meal of almost anything. Although the mouse feeds primarily on vegetables, roots, grains, seeds, and some insects for variety, he has made his home with man and has feasted on such delicacies as leather, soap, lard, paste, paper and wax.

Mice also have the ability to reproduce easily so that a population of mice is easily established. If their safety is threatened, mice will quickly settle in a new location. As the Roman dramatist Plautus observed in 190 B.C., "Consider the little mouse, how sagacious an animal it is which never entrusts its life to one hole." With danger always lurking, a mouse does not hesitate to build a nest in a new location.

Mice in the Animal World

Mice are rodents members of the order *Rodentia*. This word comes from the Latin word *rodere*, meaning "to gnaw."

SOMETHING TO GNAW ON

Mice and other rodents are known for their gnawing. Rodents are characterized by having four chisel-shaped incisors, two in the upper jaw and two in the lower jaw. These sharp teeth grow continuously throughout the animal's life. Rodents also have twelve

Mice have lived alongside man for centuries. Urban areas offer many opportunities for wild mice to get an easy meal.

molars for grinding, three on each side of the upper jaw and three on each side of the lower jaw. This arrangement of teeth allows mice to chew away at almost any kind of material. Constant chewing keeps the teeth worn down. If the teeth grow

too long, the mouse is unable to eat and will die. Thus, mice go right on chewing.

EEEK! A MOUSE (I THINK . . .)

On occasion, people find it difficult to distinguish mice from rats. Rats are generally larger than mice, usually four times as large as the little mouse. Sometimes a mouse can grow to be as large as a small rat. Rats are considered the more intelligent of the two animals and are easier to handle than the more skittish mouse. However, some people find the mouse more appealing, for the rat has a longer, pointier face and a thicker tail. Two rats commonly associated with mice are the black rat (*Rattus rattus*), also called the ship or roof rat, and the Norway rat (*Rattus norvegicus*), also called the brown, common or sewer rat.

AROUND THE GLOBE WITH MICE

Mice belong to the family *Muridae*. *Mus musculus,* the common house mouse, is a member of the subfamily *Murinae,* which includes about eighty genera of old-world mice and rats. Mice belong to the suborder *Myomorpha* (mouselike rodents). There are approximately 1,100 species of *Myomorpha.*

Mice are part of the family of animals known as Muridae.

Pet mice are considered descendants of the common house mouse (*Mus musculus*). The word "mouse" comes from the ancient Sanskrit word *musha,* which means "thief." This name attests to the longtime association between mice and man. Anthropologists believe humans and mice began living together as many as 10,000 years ago, when man domesticated both plant and animal. Mice are believed to have first settled with humans in Central Asia. As civilizations began trading, mice hid in traveling merchants' bundles and traveled to the Middle East, the Mediterranean and Europe. They were well known to the ancient Egyptians and Greeks.

Long before the rat hitched a ride with humans, the old-world mouse was already on the move. As people explored the New World, mice went with these adventurers, sailing the seas and traveling to new lands. Mice are believed to have been introduced to North America by the Spanish sailors. As voyagers settled in the faraway lands, the mice settled with them.

Different species of mice can be found in almost every corner of the world. Aside from the forty different subspecies of mice that belong to the species *Mus musculus,* other species similar to the house mouse include the white-footed deer mouse, the American harvest mouse, the cotton mouse, the kangaroo mouse, the leaf-eared mouse, the pocket mouse and the yellow-necked mouse, to name a few. Sometimes the names of these animals can be confusing. What is often referred to as the field mouse is actually a vole, which is a rodent and a cousin of the mouse. The African water rat, however, is a mouse.

Mice are found all over the world. The Zebra mouse's native habitat is in Africa.

Have You Met My Cousin?

Rodents make up 40 percent of all mammals and they are a large and varied group. There are over 1,800 species of rodents. While the majority of rodents live on land, each has the ability to climb, burrow or swim.

Some rodents, like the mouse, can do all of these activities! There are all sizes and shapes of rodents. They can be found throughout the world in almost every habitat except in the oceans and polar regions. Different physical adaptations allow these animals to survive in a variety of environments. When rodents occupy different habitats, they increase the range in which they can find food, shelter and protection. Climbing into trees for food, burrowing underground to make a home, waiting until nightfall to hunt or fleeing to water for safety are just a few of the different behavioral adaptations that profit these creatures and allow the many different types of rodents to survive.

CLIMBING SKILLS

Climbing requires great dexterity and balance, good eyesight and a firm grip. The common flying squirrel spends its life living in the trees, gliding through the night in the taigas of northern Asia. A tail gives the squirrel balance, while flexible fingers grip at the tree, penetrating the tough bark with sharp claws that allow the squirrel to climb. Big eyes give the squirrel a wide range of vision. Flying squirrels use muscles to adjust their skin into a pouch, which allows them to glide through the air at an amazing distance and look for safety and food in the Asian forest.

MY, WHAT BIG (OR SMALL) EARS YOU HAVE

Body structures, such as ears and tails, are used not only for hearing and balance, but also for heat exchange with the surrounding environment. Lemmings make their home in the frozen tundra, building a nest under the snow in winter. Their bodies are built for these harsh surroundings. Lemmings have tiny ears and short tails; this limits the amount of heat lost by the body in the cold weather. Animals that live in the desert need large ears and tails to help the body eliminate heat in these hot surroundings. The gerbil is a true desert-dwelling animal with a large nose and big ears. Gerbils also have big eyes and good vision, features that most rodents do not have.

RODENT FUR

Fur texture and coloration is another adaptation of rodents. The gerbil has a dark topcoat but has a light belly. This light coloration reflects the heat of the desert sand, protecting the little body from dehydration.

The water vole has thick fur for its life along the water's edge of North America. Thick fur insulates the vole and serves to waterproof the creature in its wet world. After the vole leaves the water, one shake of the animal can remove almost all water completely. Hair on the feet and tail also aids the vole in its swimming effort. The vole makes its home in a den in the water, opening up into the water or onto the wet bank. Another rodent that loves to swim and dive is the beaver.

The insulation provided by fur is important for rodents that live in cold climates. High in the air on mountaintops is the chinchilla, whose wide feet and long whiskers allow it to climb. But its reach is not high enough to escape man, who covets the beautiful, soft fur of the chinchilla. Not all rodents have such soft fur, though. The porcupine is one such rodent that would be difficult to hug. Spiny quills project from this rodent, protecting it from inquisitive predators.

DOES SIZE REALLY MATTER?

While most rodents are small, there are some rodents that are quite large. The largest rodent is the capybara of South America. This rodent can grow up to 4.3 feet (130 centimeters) and weigh up to 130 pounds (60 kilograms). The capybara is also called the water hog because it spends a great deal of time in the water avoiding danger. It hides in the densely vegetated bodies of water with only its nose, eyes and ears sticking out, allowing it to maintain a view of the world on land.

*The tiniest
rodent of all is
the pygmy
mouse.*

Most rodents, however, are small, usually between 3.2 and 14 inches long (8 to 35 centimeters). This small size helps rodents avoid the detection of predators. The smallest rodent is the tiny pygmy mouse, measuring less than 3 inches (7.5 centimeters), including the tail, and weighing less than $1/5$ ounce (5 to 6 grams).

Small rodents that spend most of their time on land must be quick to avoid being captured. Jumping mice, for example, have large back legs that are more powerful than their front legs. They will escape predators not on all fours, but by taking wide jumps on their hind legs. Agoutis are also good jumpers. Their strong legs allow them to jump far, and they often sit in a ready position just in case danger approaches. Agoutis are just one of many rodents that can vocalize to warn other members of their species of approaching danger.

Another such animal is the alpine marmot, who lives in the elevated regions of the Rocky Mountains about 13,000 feet high (over 4,000 meters), standing guard against predators and warning the colony of approaching danger with a piercing scream.

Oh, Baby!

Another biological difference found in various rodents is their gestation period. We know a lot about the golden hamster because it is a common pet throughout the world. This small creature has a gestation period similar to that of many other small rodents, carrying its babies for sixteen days. The endangered pacaran of the Andes in South America has a gestation period of 283 days, longer than that of a human! This peaceful creature resembles a giant guinea pig (or cavy). As its habitat is being overrun by man, this animal is at special risk—in part because its long gestation period simply impedes its ability to reproduce in adequate numbers. Although the pacaran does appear to tame easily, individuals don't live long in captivity, making its survival increasingly perilous.

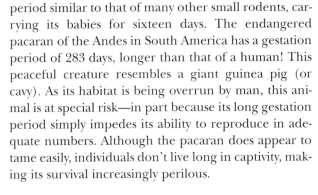

The golden hamster, another popular rodent pet, has a short gestation period, similar to that of a mouse.

HEY, IT'S DARK IN HERE

Animals living beneath the ground have evolved a special set of adaptations for underground life. The blind mole rat spends most of its life underground, digging tunnels in East Asia. It has a heavy body with strong legs. Sharp claws allow the mole rat to dig through the soil. Because it is hard to see underground, these animals rely on bristles that extend from their nose to identify objects. Like whiskers, the bristles give mole rats information about what's in front of them. The mole rat has such tiny eyes that it doesn't seem to have any at all. This rodent relies more on its hearing and sense of smell.

Another rodent, the tuco-tuco, loves to dig in the dry soils of South America. Built like the mole rat, this

13

animal will peer out of its cave, but if it senses danger, it uses its naked tail as a guide and retreats backward into its den. Another underground animal, the viscacha, is almost extinct. They were once found from southern Brazil to Patagonia but today are found only in Argentina. Local landowners are not fond of viscachas, because the animals tear up the ground with miles of subterranean tunnels.

Not Quite Rodents . . .

One group of animals that was previously classified with rodents is the lagomorphs, which include rabbits, hares and pikas. Some pikas strongly resemble mice, but they are really related to hares and rabbits. Lagomorphs are distinguished from rodents by their teeth. While the rodents have a continuously growing pair of incisors on the top and bottom of their mouths that are used for gnawing, lagomorphs have a second tooth (which looks like two separate teeth) hiding behind the upper incisors. The lagomorph also has a wider space between the teeth than rodents have. Only the lower teeth of this group grow continuously. The difference in tooth structure makes some foods more appealing to rabbits, hares and pikas than they would be to rodents.

Of Mice and Men

As a persistent member of the community, mice were forever in a struggle with man. Naturalists often pondered the position of the mouse, despising the damage done by such a small creature and yet admiring his perseverance at the same time.

The early civilizations had problems with destructive mice and considered them nuisances. Archeological excavations have uncovered mousetraps in various parts of the world. Mice are considered a pest to humans because they not only like the food we provide, but enjoy the warmth of our homes and furniture. Mice will make their homes in anything from barns and cellars to upholstered chairs and cabinetry.

They will gnaw at almost any type of material and have been blamed for damage done to buildings and electrical wires. Food left unattended is readily consumed. Millions of dollars of crops have been destroyed, not only from the gnawing of the mouse, but also from the urine and feces of these pests that contaminate grains and feed, making these foods unusable for livestock and humans.

MICE AS PESTS

Mice are also considered pests because they can carry disease. In the fourteenth century, China and Europe were ravaged by the bubonic plague, also known as the Black Death. The plague was caused by *Yersinia pestis,* bacteria carried by infected fleas that would travel in the fur of mice and rats. Fleas would jump off the rodent and bite humans, spreading the virus. The disease reduced the population of China by 30 percent and killed about 40 million Europeans. Although the spread of the disease was the result of fleas, the mouse still bears much of the blame.

Although we enjoy mice as pets today, the mouse's relationship with mankind has not always been friendly.

Today, disease from mice is still a threat. The airborne Hantavirus is a deadly lung disease that is transmitted to humans through the urine and feces of an infected deer mouse. People who work in areas where infected wild mice have built nests can accidentally inhale particles if they disturb the nest. Scientists are concerned that humans may also be able to ingest the virus if they eat or drink products contaminated by diseased rodents.

Different civilizations had different methods for combating mice. One was the cat, domesticated by Egyptian society to extinguish mice. The Bible tells of

15

God sending a plague of mice upon the Philistines, who had stolen the Ark of the Covenant from the Jews. To protect themselves from God's wrath, the Philistines returned the ark with a gilt offering of five golden mice as an apology from each leader of the Philistine people.

Seventh-century Irish poets specialized in poetry intended to cast out mice. This poetry was believed to have the ability to control mice and other animals. A poem by Senchan was credited with causing ten mice to drop dead in his presence after they consumed an egg he had been saving.

Saint Gertrude was the patron saint of mouse and rat catchers. She is celebrated for having expelled swarms of mice and is depicted in art with mice running all over her. In early America, women who kept mice as pets were accused of witchcraft. The mice were believed to be instruments of the devil.

MICE TO BE PRAISED

Mickey Mouse is worshipped all over the world. © Walt Disney Pictures

On the other hand, some ancient societies worshipped mice. Ancient Egyptians might have wanted to be rid of mice, but they also believed that mice were born from the mud of the Nile and, through this birth, had healing properties.

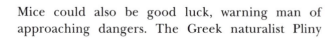
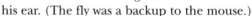

Other societies believed mice could cure diseases, including measles, whooping cough and small pox. Man benefited from mice in other ways as well. Saint Colman was believed to travel with a rooster, a mouse and a fly. The mouse served as a snooze button on the alarm clock. The rooster woke the saint, but if Saint Colman wanted to sleep a little longer, the mouse would nibble at his ear. (The fly was a backup to the mouse.)

Mice could also be good luck, warning man of approaching dangers. The Greek naturalist Pliny credited mice with prophecy, observing around the second century A.D., "When the building is about to fall down, all the mice desert it." In "To a Mouse," the eighteenth-century poet Robert Burns reflected that mice and humans were alike, for life does not happen as we expect: "The best laid schemes of mice and men often go astray."

Mouse Legends and Myths: Mice in the Media

Despite our supposed fear of mice, these creatures transcend almost every medium of entertainment. They can be found in books, magazines, comic strips, on television, in greeting cards, in the ballet and theater and may even have their own internet sites. Generally, mice are portrayed in a positive light.

MICE IN CARTOONS
Disney Mice

Mickey Mouse is undoubtedly the world's most recognizable mouse. The Walt Disney star has been translated into almost every language imaginable. This happy-go-lucky mouse has seen adventure and faced danger, battled ghosts, pirates, and crazed scientists. He is a good friend and a snazzy dresser, but is not to be trusted with a magic wand, as we learned in "The Sorcerer's Apprentice" segment of *Fantasia*—Mickey almost drowns himself when he cannot stop the brooms and their buckets of water.

Mickey Mouse made his screen debut on November 18, 1928, in the animated cartoon *Steamboat Willie.* Less than two years later, on January 13, 1930, Mickey Mouse appeared in comic strips in the adventure *Lost on*

MICKEY AROUND THE WORLD

Mickey Mouse is known throughout the world. In most languages his name is the same or similar, such as Micky, Miki or Mike. Variations from different countries include:

China	Mi Lao Shu
Finland	Mikki Hiiri
Indonesia	Miki Tikus
Italy	Topolino
Spain	El Ratón Mickey
Sweden	Musse Pigg

Despite the different translations, Mickey Mouse is always recognizable!

a Desert Island, where we met his lovely friend Minnie Mouse. From the initial introduction, Mickey Mouse has become a family favorite throughout the world.

Other mice are also featured in Walt Disney productions that included twists to classic stories and tales.

Dumbo (1941), the story of an outcast baby elephant with big ears, features Timothy Mouse, who befriends the sad elephant. Dumbo learns to fly, flapping his ears and becoming the star of the circus. Timothy Mouse becomes Dumbo's manager, signing a prestigious Hollywood contract. The animated film *Cinderella* (1950) features Jacques and Gus, two of Cinderella's animal friends whose friendship keeps her in good spirits despite her troubling tasks.

Tom and Jerry were (almost) the best of friends. (Courtesy of Photofest)

The 1951 classic *Alice in Wonderland* features an animal often thought of as a mouse: the little dormouse. The mad tea party would not be complete without this sleepy attendee. More recent additions to the Disney family include Bernard and Miss Bianca of *The Rescuers* (1977). This Disney film is based on the novels by Margery Sharp and follows Bernard and Miss Bianca as they rescue young Penny from the evil Madame Medusa, who is holding Penny in the swampy Devil's Bayou. The heroic mice later find themselves in Australia where they're joined by Frank and Esmerelda in *The Rescuers Down Under* (1990).

Although Disney has brought us many delightful movie mice, it doesn't have a monopoly on the cartoon mouse. The singing mice of the popular movie *Babe* and its sequel, *Babe: Pig in the City,* narrate the stories in little voices that are truly unforgettable. *Mouse Hunt* is the story of Ernie and Lars Smuntz, who are brought together by the little mouse that invades their late father's home. The mouse saves them from financial ruin when he shows them how to convert their string factory into a cheese factory. The Smuntz brothers reward the clever mouse by making him the official cheese taster.

OTHER CARTOON MICE

Animated mice can be spotted in movies featuring human actors. Jerry Mouse of the pair Tom & Jerry had his own dance scene with the legendary Gene Kelly in *Anchors Aweigh* (1944). Both Tom and Jerry swim alongside the beautiful Esther Williams in *Dangerous When Wet* (1953). Tom & Jerry debuted in the 1933 MGM production of *Puss Gets the Boot.* This Hanna–Barbera team relied on music and sound effects instead of speech to keep the story rolling.

Here I come to save the day! (Mighty Mouse photo courtesy of Photofest)

Yet another cartoon favorite in the early 1940s was Mighty Mouse of Terrytoons fame. Originally designed as a lampoon of Superman, Mighty Mouse gained an audience of his own. He can still be seen in reruns today, saving the day as he rescues mice from the evil cats.

Also in reruns is Speedy Gonzales, the fastest mouse in all of Mexico. This Warner Brothers' darling was ever helpful to mice everywhere, appearing in his starched white outfit and sombrero with a red handkerchief tied around his neck, leaving a cloud of dust in his wake.

LITERARY MICE
Children's Books

Mice have long been favorite fictional characters. They often make their way into fables and nursery rhymes. The mouse of Aesop's ancient fable *The Lion and the Mouse* entertains a lion that accidentally traps the little mouse under his paw while the great King of the Beasts is napping. The mouse promises to assist the lion at a later date if the lion lets her go. The amused lion is later rewarded when he becomes ensnared in a trap and the mouse gnaws him free, proving that friends of any size can come to your aid.

Mice in nursery rhymes include the Hickory Dickory Dock mouse that gets exercise running up and down the clock, and the three blind mice that make the mistake of frightening the farmer's wife.

In the stories of Beatrix Potter, the author provides children with heroes and heroines of all shapes and size, including quite a few talented mice. In Potter's version of *The Tailor of Gloucester* (1903), it is two helpful mice who save the tailor's day. When the tailor sends his cat Simpkin to purchase thread, he releases Simpkin's dinner—two little mice dressed in the leftovers of the tailors scraps. The tailor then goes to bed, ill with fever and unable to finish the waistcoat he is sewing for the mayor, who is getting married the next day. To reward the tailor for his kindness, the mice creep out and do all of the work except for one little button hole, for they had no more thread.

In the *Tale of Two Bad Mice* (1904), Tom Thumb and Hunca Munca break into a dollhouse when the owners are away. Hungry for food, clothing and furniture, the duo make a mess of the dollhouse, destroying the contents of every room, both upstairs and down. They are discovered by the dolls at the height of their burglary, but repay the owners for the destruction. Tom Thumb finds a coin that he gives them, and each morning Hunca Munca comes and sweeps out the dollhouse.

The Tale of Johnny Town Mouse (1918) is derived from Aesop's fable of the country mouse and the city mouse. In this retelling, Johnny Town Mouse is having a dinner party, which is interrupted by the unexpected arrival of his friend Timmy Willie from the garden. Johnny tries to make Timmy feel at home, but the loud noises, strange foods and presence of a cat in the house are much too much for the little mouse, who longs to return to the garden. With his departure, Johnny promises to visit him in the garden. But upon arriving in the garden, Johnny finds the garden too damp and the place too quiet, and immediately returns home.

Other Beatrix Potter favorites include little Appley Dapply, who runs away with sweets from people's cupboards. Poor Mrs. Thomasina Tittlemouse is bothered by uninvited and ungracious guests. And the teasing little mouse who bothered Miss Moppet (sister of Tom Kitten) is taught a lesson as she tosses him in the air in a kerchief before he escapes from the annoyed cat.

There are a wealth of other authors who were inspired by the sharpness of mice. For example, E. B. White's wonderful *Stuart Little* captured the hearts of many. When Stuart, a fine little mouse, was born to his human family, he was quite a surprise. Stuart grew into a small but helpful and courteous member of the family, often assisting his mother in retrieving her lost jewelry. Stuart had many friends, human and animal alike, which was due mainly to his pleasant nature and belief that one should always pay his own way and be nice to others.

Mrs. Frisby of *Mrs. Frisby and the Rats of NIMH* is a courageous mouse that relies on the rats living under Mr. Fitzgibbon's rosebush. In seeking their help to move her sickly son, she learns that the rats escaped from the National Institute of Mental Health where her late husband had also been imprisoned. Both her husband and the rats had received injections of serum that increased their ability to learn. What the rats soon discover is that she is as helpful to them as they are to her.

Children have also long enjoyed Anatole of picture-book fame and Basil the mouse detective, both created by Eve Titus.

Mice in Adult Literature

Adult fiction includes the exploits of clever mice. In Douglas Adams' *Hitchhiker's Guide to the Galaxy*, Arthur

Dent discovers that the planet Earth is actually a huge computer program paid for by mice, in which they run around in wheels, conducting subtle experiments on humans. The mice are extremely upset when the Earth is blown up by Vogons to make way for a bypass to the interstellar highway.

Mice on Stage

Pyotr Ilich Tchaikovsky's magnificent musical score brings to life the E. T. A. Hoffmann tale of the handsome Nutcracker and the evil Mouse King. On Christmas Eve, young Clara dreams of her home as the battleground between the two. She awakens to find that the family Christmas tree and all other objects have grown to gigantic proportions, including the Nutcracker. The Mouse King seizes Clara and tries to kidnap her, only to be defeated and killed by the handsome Nutcracker. When she awakens on Christmas day, Clara discovers it was all a wonderful dream—one she had because her bothersome brother, Fritz, scared her with a tiny little mouse earlier that day.

Contributions to Humanity
MICE AND MEDICINE

Scientists spend hours developing and testing theories that potentially allowed us to live longer, healthier lives. Mice make up the largest number of vertebrate animals used to test these theories and have been invaluable to man in research. So much of what seems obvious to us now is actually information we have recently learned, thanks to mice.

Experiments with mice have been important to our understanding of deadly diseases and viruses, including AIDS, the effects of aging, Alzheimer's disease, blood disorders, many types of cancer, cystic fibrosis, heart attacks, Huntington's disease, leukemia, neurological diseases, pediatric syndromes, the use of steroids, stress, tissue repair and ulcers, just to name a few. Studying the effects of these diseases allows scientists to develop treatments and cures, which then have to be studied as well. These advances would not be possible without the mouse.

Why Use Mice?

Mice are invaluable in research because they are similar to humans in many ways. For example, their immune systems react to disease just as ours do. This similarity allows scientists to better understand and interpret human reactions and how mutations affect

We have the little mouse to thank for great strides in medical research.

us. Mice are also easy to handle. They reproduce quickly and mature early. Researchers can study the lifetime effects of diseases and treatments, but in a much shorter period of time than scientists who work with longer-living animals. Mice are small, so scientists can work with large numbers and get more reliable information.

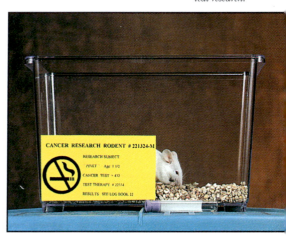

CANCER RESEARCH RODENT # 221324-M

RESEARCH SUBJECT

MALE   Age 1 1/2

CANCER TEST # 412

TEST THERAPY # 22114

RESULTS SEE LOG BOOK 22

How Do We Treat Mice?

Many people who work in laboratories believe that mice need to be treated with respect and concern. The Health Research Extension Act of 1985 is one law designed to protect mice and other animals in research settings. There are animal rights activists who would argue that laws do not go far enough. Other activists contest the use of any animal in research for human benefit. These activists have different beliefs, but as a result of their attention, more effort has been placed on the humane treatment of animals.

MICE AND ECOLOGY

The heated debate over the use of animals for human benefit continues, but all people recognize the role of the mouse in the ecological balance. The food web (sometimes referred to as a food chain) is divided into sections called trophic, or nutritional, levels, and mice occupy an important place.

At the primary level are the green plants, or the organisms that produce their own food through photosynthesis. They are eaten by consumers at the second level, such as mice. The mice that farmers consider to be so harmful actually do them good—mice love to dine on insects that would cause even more destruction to crops.

Mice, in turn, make up a great part of the diet of many birds, reptiles and mammals. The absence of mice would have an immediate impact on those animals and humans. For example, a hungry predator would be just as happy to take a farmer's chicken as he would to eat a little mouse. Just as a captive mouse requires his natural nutrition in a domestic setting, mice are routinely sold as food for other domesticated pets, such as snakes, and to preservation societies that house birds of prey, such as owls and falcons. And so, mice are extremely important in the overall cycle of life.

LAND-LOVING RODENTS

Rodents that live on land need water and must always have an adequate supply. The common Norway rat can be spotted in cities, running in the New York subway system as if to catch the next train. Finding both water and food is easy for this clever rodent. By making its home alongside man, the rat takes advantage of the waters of the sewer systems and the leftovers of the city.

chapter 2

Mice as Pets

Mice make wonderful pets. These loving little creatures add to your life in a number of ways. They are affordable, both to purchase and to maintain. They take up little space and can fit into the smallest apartment or home. And unlike fish, another common apartment pet, mice can be held and cuddled. Mice will adapt easily to new situations.

Mice are extremely tidy; and although they occasionally give off an unpleasant odor, this is usually the result of their owners' failure to change their bedding. While mice require consistent care, they are undemanding, unlike barking dogs and cats that scratch the furniture. When they become tame, mice are great friends. They are easy to care for and fun to watch. A number of mice housed together in a large cage can be observed for hours as they play and groom. Studies have shown that pets like mice lower our blood pressure and reduce tension by allowing us to relax and smile, which adds serenity to our hectic lives.

Appreciating the Active Mouse

The more we know about the amusement mice provide, the more we can appreciate them. These alert, adaptive creatures are fun to watch and more fun to play with. Place a piece of bread and a mouse in your hand and watch her discover the delicious treat. As she sits in your palm and nibbles away, you can delight in the little hands moving their way over the bread, the whiskers twitching with excitement, the mouth working furiously to finish this tasty find.

Place ropes or ladders in the cage and watch the mice run along, wrapping their tails around the ropes for extra balance. With their hearts beating at an awesome rate, mice have lots of energy, but they also need lots of sleep. Although they are awake during the day and night, these little animals are generally nocturnal. Awaken one slowly and watch her jump to attention, scrub away at her little face with her paws to make it clean and shiny and be ready to eat or play.

Mice can be timid until properly socialized, which requires frequent handling and touching of the soft fur. These pets love classical music, so put some on and watch them come alive. Place a cardboard roll in the cage and soon the roll is gone as the mouse chews holes to make a hiding spot, pushing and pulling bedding in and out, making a little nest.

Is a Mouse Right for You?

It's easy to get excited about having a mouse for a pet and watching all of the fun described above. But how do you know that a mouse is the right pet for you? As with caring for any pet, becoming a mouse owner requires you to be a dynamic partner in this little creature's life. Keeping mice is usually a fairly simple task, requiring cleaning, feeding and a short amount of time each day to interact with your little friend. But these tasks require consistency. Not all people have the time that it takes. Mice are social creatures. They will depend on you not only for basic necessities, but also for companionship and interaction.

Although they cost less than a dog or cat, mice still require love and attention. It is easier to ignore a little creature locked away in a cage than it is to ignore a pet that walks up to you and demands attention, so you must remember your small friend. The information below is given not to dissuade you from acquiring a mouse, but rather to help you decide whether this is a good decision for you.

> ### MICE AS PETS: PROS AND CONS
>
> **PROS**
>
> - affordable and easy to keep
> - affectionate and cuddly
> - don't take up much space
> - fun to play with
> - interesting to watch (which keeps us healthy, too)
>
> **CONS**
>
> - distinct odor
> - need daily attention
> - extremely prolific
> - short life span

Mice are quite social. Your attention is especially important if you keep only one mouse.

There are some drawbacks to mice as pets that one should keep in mind. Mice are more timid than their ratty cousins. The distinct odor of mice is more prominent in males than in females, but odor can be controlled by regularly cleaning the cage. Mice are incredibly prolific and can reproduce in great numbers. When keeping mice, you must keep males and females separated in order to avoid an unwanted population explosion. Mice have a short life span, averaging between 1½ to 3 years. It can be difficult to lose a friend you have had for such a short period of time. Despite these inconveniences, however, the active and sensitive nature of mice makes them a pet worth having for many people.

OWNER'S RESPONSIBILITIES

Consider the following questions before purchasing your mouse:

- **Why do you want a mouse?**

  The decision to purchase a mouse should be made after doing some research so you understand the responsibilities involved. Is this a pet you will enjoy throughout her entire life, or is getting a mouse your whim of the week?

- **Do you have time each day to attend to your mouse?**

  Even thirty minutes a day will give your mouse the time she needs with you. During this time you can enjoy your pet while giving her a view of the world outside her cage. Are you able to provide this attention?

- **Can you provide the proper maintenance that your mouse needs?**

  Mice need not only food and toys, but also daily and weekly housekeeping. Because they are small, sensitive creatures, mice require the strictest care in this regard. Are you able to set aside time each day to feed your pet and check her cage?

- **Will your pet have a space of her own?**

  Giving your mouse a home includes allocating a specific space for your pet. This must be a place where she can see you and you can see her. Mice are extremely susceptible to changes in temperature, to drafts and to direct light. Do you have a place where you can protect your pet, yet give her the proper quality of life she deserves?

- **Are you ready for a pet that will have such a short life span?**

Losing a beloved pet is never an easy thing, and this can be especially intense if you have your pet for less than two years. Can you accept losing a pet that you have so recently acquired?

- **Do you have someone to care for your pet when you are not around?**

Properly caring for a pet means making sure someone is always available to look after the pet when you're away. Do you have family or friends who are not frightened by this small creature and who are willing to provide the interaction your pet will surely miss if you are gone?

- **Do you have other pets or children that will interact with the mouse?**

Young children and other pets can be dangerous to a little mouse. Small children do not realize the physical pressure they can exert. Curious dogs and cats can injure your new pet. Do you have a system in place to protect a mouse from the other members of your family?

- **Will you be able to interact with your pet and play with her?**

Mice in the wild live in colonies. They are social creatures that require attention, especially when living alone. Can you give the time to your mouse that she will require? Will you not only change food, water and bedding, but also handle and play with your new friend?

MOUSE ESSENTIALS

To keep your mouse healthy, she'll need:

- a clean and safe home
- room to exercise
- a well-balanced diet of pellets and small treats
- fresh drinking water daily

To keep your mouse happy, she'll need:

- toys to play with
- friends to cuddle next to
- someone to scratch her head
- your attention and affection

- **Does everyone in the family want the pet?**

  Is this a decision that everyone agrees to, or is one opinion louder than all the rest? A mouse will need consistent love and attention. There must be a commitment on everyone's part so that the little mouse is not neglected. Is everyone in favor of keeping a mouse?

- **Will you respond to your pet with medical attention if the need should arise?**

  Even with the best of care, mice can require medical attention. Will you choose a veterinarian ahead of time and pay strict attention to your mouse's habits, taking your mouse to the veterinarian if suggested or required?

CHILDREN AND MICE

Before choosing to share your life with a mouse, discuss the decision with the other members of the family. A mouse can be a great pet for a child 8 years old or older, as it gives a child a fuzzy friend with which to bond.

Before bringing a mouse or mice home, talk about how each child sees the mouse fitting in with the family. Does each child understand the responsibility involved as well as the fun? Do they understand that it is better if the mouse stays in a common area where everyone can enjoy her instead of in a bedroom where the mouse might be overlooked?

Some parents choose to purchase a mouse to teach their child the obligations involved in caring for a pet. Before doing so, it's very important for you to be comfortable that the child is ready, willing and able to succeed. Moreover, you must be prepared to step in if the child fails to actively look after the mouse. Ask yourself, does the child care for other living things already in the household (a dog, a cat, a plant)? Assess your child's strengths and weaknesses before buying a pet. Does the child care for his personal belongings properly? Does he understand that mice are small, fragile creatures that must be treated gently and cannot be handled roughly? Discuss how accidents occur. Talk about different things each person can do to make sure the mouse stays safe.

Explain that if an accident should occur, the child should come to you immediately, no matter what happened to the mouse or how it occurred. The welfare of the mouse is the most important detail in owning a pet. Explain that mice can get tired, just as people do, and that certain types of play are just as inappropriate for small animals as they are for larger ones. Children will learn to recognize what is appropriate activity with guidance.

Children can learn to interact appropriately with the fragile mouse.

Generally, mice are not good pets for young children under the age of 8. At about 8 years, children have developed the dexterity and coordination to hold a mouse. Mice, unlike other pet rodents, will bite if they feel threatened. Most young children do not understand when they are exerting too much pressure. A child may not mean to squeeze the mouse tightly or hurt the mouse, but a mouse bites when unsure. The alarmed child then reacts predictably by dropping the mouse, and this situation turns into an unfortunate encounter for everyone. If you have young children and choose a mouse for a pet, always supervise when the mouse is out of the cage.

Scheduling time for the mouse to come out of the cage each day will be helpful to the child and the mouse.

This consistency teaches the child that pets require daily attention and gives the mouse an opportunity for affection. Stroking and cuddling with the mouse increases the child's attachment to the mouse while providing the community mice have in the wild. When it's time for daily and weekly chores, include the child in this activity. While the adult washes the cage, the child can wash the toys or the food dish. When the adult is putting the water in the cage, the child can fill the food bowl. Making this activity fun maintains the child's interest in both the responsibility of caring for and the joy of having a pet mouse. The following guidelines can make sharing a mouse with a younger child a pleasurable experience for everyone.

Eleven Easy Safety Tips for Children and Mice

1. **Ask adult permission to take the mouse out of her cage.** Make it clear to the child that the pet can only come out of the cage with permission. Some children may interpret this to mean asking any adult that is handy. It must be emphasized that the adult is to be someone who will stay and watch the child while the child is playing with the mouse.

Teach your child to handle a mouse very gently.

2. **Stay within sight of an adult, who must always supervise play.** This means keeping the mouse where an adult can observe activity. Children are not to take the mouse into the bedroom. It is difficult for parents to watch every little thing their

child is doing, so the mouse should stay in the cage if the adult is distracted by other obligations. By choosing a time during the day when the mouse comes out of the cage, this can be an opportunity for everyone to share some time together.

3. **Stay seated with the mouse.** Do not walk or run with the mouse. Small rodents move quickly and get scared easily if they are not yet tamed. An accidental fall, even from the hands of a child who is close to the ground, can greatly harm the mouse. Choose a seat ahead of time, such as the couch or a large chair. Walk there slowly and sit down carefully. Even a tame mouse requires gentle handling.

4. **Children may not put the mouse on the floor.** Mice are curious creatures and will want to explore everything. Each opportunity a mouse has to travel farther away from her cage, the more self-reliant she becomes. Even tame mice will run away if the opportunity presents itself. Not placing the mouse on the floor prevents the mouse from getting lost or stepped on.

5. **Children may not take the mouse out of the house—even to show the neighbor.** If your child would like to introduce the mouse to someone, invite the guest into your home, but do not take the mouse outside. It is complicated enough to recapture an escaped mouse that is hiding behind a refrigerator. Once free in the outside world, you are almost assured the mouse is gone. The lost pal then runs the risk of being attacked by predators, such as a neighborhood cat.

6. **Children may not play with another pet while the mouse is enjoying time out of the cage.** Little mice can become the victims of a hungry dog or cat that sees them as a tasty treat. Mice have many natural predators, including birds and other rodents. When playing with the pet mouse, make sure she is in an isolated area away from other pets.

7. **Children may not engage in dangerous play with the mouse.** Children sometimes see a pet as a toy and not as a living creature. They assume the

mouse can be handled the same way a doll or toy
solider can be handled. Swinging the mouse in the
air to make her fly or squeezing the mouse into a
small container is as dangerous as it is inappropriate. While mice do like to hide, children should
not put them in a place where the pet could be for-
gotten or suffocate or in anything from which
there is no easy exit, such as a lidded box. There
are toys designed specifically for mice to be placed
in, but be sure to supervise the child so that no
harm comes to the mouse.

8. **Children must be cautious with clothing items.** The
   idea of dressing your mouse or placing the mouse
   in your own clothing can be appealing, but doll
   clothing can cause a mouse injury if her little legs
   are forced into outfits. Putting a ribbon around
   the mouse's neck may look cute, but could choke
   the mouse. While adult clothing is designed to be
   roomier, some children like to put mice into their
   own pockets, which can be too tight for the mouse.
   Use caution with these items.

*Children can
have fun simply
observing a
mouse in her
cage.*

9. **Watch where you sit!** Mice move quickly, and it is
   easy to sit on a mouse. Even a child is large compared to this small creature. If you stand up to let
   the mouse run on the chair or sofa, pick the
   mouse up again before sitting down a second time.

10. **Children may not give the mouse a bath.** Mice are fastidious when it comes to grooming themselves. It is quite rare that a mouse needs a bath. Should the need arise, this is a job for an adult.

11. **Children are to treat the mouse gently.** Pet mice can be accidentally injured in various ways, sometimes with dire consequences. The best way to avoid any such occurrence is to remember that this is a fragile animal that requires gentle handling and consideration. Make sure that a child treats the mouse like the delicate animal she is and respects her abilities.

It's important that older children also understand that a mouse is not a toy, but a friend who merits respect. While older children are more comfortable handling a mouse and playing with her, they also must use wise judgment. Running around or taking the mouse out of the home unprotected are not good ideas, even for older children.

Mice and Visitors

When friends come to visit, the last thing they expect is to be caught unaware by a mouse. Although we see a delightful and sweet creature, some people see vermin with nervous twittering and an icky tail. Always ask someone if they would like to meet your tiny friend before you automatically introduce them. Not doing so can cause injury to your mouse and to your relationship with your guest. Invite your guest to first pet your mouse in the cage, or while you are holding her. This allows your mouse to get used to your friend's scent and your friend to your mouse's movements. Show the guest how you hold and carry the mouse before allowing him to do so if he has not been exposed to these animals before this occasion. Some people may prefer to observe you enjoying your mouse or they may have no interest at all. Some people may even fear the mouse and choose to leave the room when she is present. Whatever the situation, your visitor's wishes should be respected.

chapter 3

Understanding
Your
Mouse

Mice love to run, jump, climb and hide. In captivity they are much less active than they are in nature and may become bored without stimulation. These tiny creatures require activity because their little bodies are designed to be animated, to move and look for food, to live in a community and interact with other mice and to hide and play. Mice in captivity have been bred to be more tame than wild mice, but you may be surprised to learn that even pet mice retain part of their native ancestry.

The Secretive Mouse

Have you ever known someone who thinks they have a mouse in their cupboards, but can't quite find one? They might find some small droppings or a tiny hole, but these are the only clues to the mouse's presence. The inconspicuous mouse is gifted with the ability to avoid detection. This ability enables the mouse to survive in a variety of places and has allowed the mouse to travel across continents, hiding in the belongings of humans as they see the world. His small size, specialized behaviors and fertility assure the mouse that he will be successful in conquering any area he decides to call home.

Mouse Anatomy

BODY

A full-grown mouse is only 6 inches long. He has a 3-inch body, a 3-inch tail and weighs about 1 ounce. This small size conceals the mouse from the gaze of many larger animals. Mice are agile climbers and move quickly, allowing them to dart off before being noticed. If danger approaches, the little mouse can hide in the tiniest of cracks to avoid detection. Sharp teeth help the mouse gnaw through almost all materials, so the mouse can hide anywhere, such as a kitchen cabinet or a fluffy upholstered chair or a little space in the wall.

A well-developed central nervous system is adapted to react quickly to events in the environment. Big ears aid in the mouse's excellent hearing. Fine-tuned senses keep the little mouse alert. With a tiny body and a fast-beating heart, the little mouse eats small meals throughout the day to get enough energy, but does not surpass the offerings of his environment.

HAIR

Hair is one of the defining characteristics of mammals, although we humans are not very hairy. Hair serves mammals in many ways. It protects the skin from sizzling sun and pouring rain. It insulates the body from changing temperatures. Colors in a coat help an animal blend into the surroundings.

Mice have two kinds of hair: fur and whiskers. The fur is hair that covers the body. Two kinds of fur, underhair and guard hair, make up a coat. Underhair is thick and soft, insulating the mouse during changing temperatures. The underhair is protected by the long guard hairs. These guard hairs give the mouse his coloration, which provides him with a camouflage in the wilderness. The coat will be thinner in the summer and thicker in the winter, when the body needs more insulation. Most mice of the species *Mus musculus* have a grayish-brown coat. The underbelly is usually a lighter version of the topcoat. Mice that live outdoors may have a more golden hue.

WHISKERS

We expect a mouse to fit into a tiny hole, but how does a mouse know he will fit? A mouse relies on his whiskers! Whiskers, or vibrissae, are stiff hairs that project from the face of the mouse. These sensitive protrusions allow the mouse to navigate, especially in the dark. The mouse uses his whiskers to feel out territory. The base of each whisker is connected to a sensory nerve in the skin. Each time the whisker is moved, signals are sent to the brain telling the mouse about his surroundings. The brain then lets the mouse know if he will fit into holes and spaces.

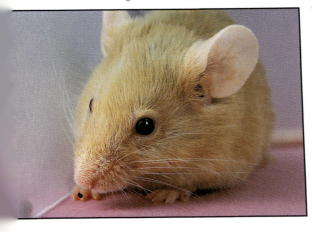

A mouse's sensitive whiskers tell him all about his surroundings.

FEET

Mice are extremely agile, in large measure due to their flexible feet. These feet can easily grip objects and have various uses, including climbing, running, fighting, eating and constructing nests. Mice have well-developed limbs that allow them to manage materials when they build their nests. Mice have four toes on each of the front feet and five toes on each of the rear feet. When you watch a mouse eat, you will see him hold onto the food and grip it, turning it about for a better angle. Little nails extend from each toe, allowing the mouse to grip onto surfaces and increasing his climbing and running agility.

TAIL

A mouse's tail is adapted for grasping, support and balance. The flexible tail is made up of multiple rings stacked in a thin row. It is almost naked, its scaly skin sparsely covered with small hairs. The tail is approximately the same length as the body. A mouse uses his tail by swinging it back and forth or curling it around objects. You may notice the tail curling around

your finger when you hold your little friend or see him twist the tail around a rope he's scaling. Mice who try to escape a predator can lose a portion of the tail. If the tail is injured or amputated, a mouse's ability to maneuver will likely be compromised.

A mouse will use his tail for support while climbing.

TEETH

Most mammals have heterodontal teeth, which are different types of teeth for different purposes. Humans have incisors for biting, canines for tearing, premolars for crushing and grinding and molars for grinding larger pieces of food. Mice have sixteen teeth consisting of only incisors and molars. There are two upper incisors and two lower incisors, which grow continuously. Mice grind their teeth together to keep them sharp. These razor-sharp teeth can gnaw through almost any material. Teeth are covered with enamel, which protects the teeth. In the back of the mouth there are twelve molars, six in the upper jaw and six in the lower jaw. These teeth are used for grinding. Mice have no canine teeth, so there is a gap between the incisors and the molars called the diastema. This gap allows mice to suck in their cheeks, blocking off the entrance to their throat and protecting their throat from harmful items as they gnaw.

MOUSE FACTS

Size: 6 inches including tail

Weight: From $^2/_5$ ounce to 1 ounce

Average Life Span: $1\frac{1}{2}$ to 3 years

Age at Puberty: 6 weeks

Breeding Season: Females cycle every 4 to 5 days

Gestation Period: 19 to 21 days

Litter Size: 1 to 12 babies (5 is average)

Weaning Age: 3 weeks

Identity: Males—bucks; females—does; young—cubs

Defining Characteristics: 2 pairs of ever-growing incisors that can gnaw through almost anything. Agile climbers, able gnawers, and escape artists

PHEROMONES

Mice communicate with one another through visual, auditory and chemical signals. One very strong chemical signal is that produced by pheromones. Pheromones are chemical substances released by the body that give signals to other mice. These odors are very important in a mouse's life. The presence of pheromones stimulates other mice to behave in inborn ways. Mice recognize one another because of these odors, which are secreted from a number of places, such as the feet, the face and the base of the tail.

Signaling pheromones advertise to males and females that it is time to mate. The scent is used to mark territory and to warn off intruding mice. Priming pheromones can block pregnancy in dense populations. Scientists believe that these hormones, when secreted by the dominant male mouse (buck), increase the ability of young females to mate and suppress the ability of competing males. This allows the dominant mouse to maintain his position and serves as a sort of population control within the colony.

Gestation and Babies

Reproductive behavior occurs so frequently in such a short span of time that the mouse population can survive even if the majority of the litter is lost to death and predators. The female mouse (doe), will give birth nineteen to twenty-one days after becoming pregnant. Newborns are often referred to as "pinkies" because of their pink, translucent skin. They are born blind and hairless in an underdeveloped condition with their eyes and ears closed. These immature babies are dependent upon their mothers until they develop. There can be as few as one and as many as twelve babies in a litter, but mice generally have five or six young at one time. Hair begins to grow after three days, and the ears and eyes open after ten days. In about two weeks they look like tiny adults. Young mice are often referred to as cubs.

Only 8 days old, these baby mice have yet to open their eyes.

GROWING UP

Mice are weaned and ready to eat solid food less than three weeks after they are born. They are considered adults at about 6 weeks of age, full-grown at 12 weeks of age, and elderly as early as 1 year. They can begin breeding at a mere 8 weeks. Mice in the wild can have several litters a year, and a mouse in captivity or hiding in your home can reproduce almost once a month! When they are adults, females will weigh between 20 and 40 grams and males between 22 and 63 grams.

Senses

Survival in the wild demands that mice have fine-tuned senses. These alert creatures will react immediately if they perceive danger, scurrying quickly for cover.

SIGHT

A mouse's vision is not his sensory strength. The eye collects the information and sends it to the brain.

There are different structures within the eye that allow
this activity. In the mouse's eye, the cornea focuses the
image in the retina. The retina is made up of photore-
ceptors called rods and cones, which pick out distinc-
tions in the surroundings. Cones detect fine points
and images. Rods detect shades, outlines of forms and
shadows. Rods are especially useful in dim light, such
as dawn, dusk and nighttime—times when the mouse
is more active. It is then not surprising to learn that the
mouse has a greater quantity of rods than of cones, limiting the mouse's perception of color. A mouse generally perceives the world as black and white. Large
round eyes give the mouse a wide range of view. The
shape of the eye allows the little mouse to freeze when
being watched by a predator, keeping tabs on the danger without turning his head, which would let the
predator know his location.

SMELL

The ability to detect scents is one of a mouse's most
valuable tools. When animals are sniffing the air, they
are actually distinguishing between many different
molecules around them. Humans do not rely on their
sense of smell as much as a little mouse does, as the
human sense of smell is not nearly as acute. With his
fine attention to scents, a mouse is able to detect if an
approaching mouse is friend or foe. The sharp sense of
smell also allows the mouse to find food. Once food is
discovered, mice love to bury it until they are hungry
again. Without this keen sense of smell, mice would be
unable to find their buried food supply. When estab-
lishing a new home, mice rely on the scents around
them to decide if another colony of mice has already
settled the area.

HEARING

With so many predators on the prowl for a mouse, this
small creature must be able hear them coming! The
ear detects the intensity and frequency of sound. The
frequency of sound is expressed as cycles per second,
or Hertz (Hz). Humans perceive sounds in the range

of 1500 to 3000 Hz. Most other mammals perceive sound in a range of about 20,000 Hz. But mice have ultrasonic hearing and ultrasonic communication. They hear sounds occurring between 1000 and 100,000 Hz. This means mice hear sounds that exist at a frequency twenty-five times greater than our own hearing! Because of a mouse's excellent hearing, successful predators must move virtually without a sound. This extraordinary hearing is one reason we rarely hear mice converse (they don't need to shout!) and why high-pitched appliances in the home can stress your mouse. When baby mice are separated from their mothers, their squeaky cries bring the mother running to their rescue.

Behaviors

Wild mice live in colonies. Territory is established and marked with the scent of the mice. A "lead" male will head the colony with a few females, a few submissive males and the young. Only the dominant male is able to mate with the females, which is one way in which the population is controlled. This community usually stays intact until a more aggressive male tries to assert his dominance or until mice establish another colony. Within the colony, mice engage in a variety of behaviors based around this living structure.

AGGRESSION

Aggression is usually the direct result of one male trying to assert dominance over the lead buck. The two males will fight and the winner becomes (or remains) the head of the colony. Mice usually do not fight to the death. A losing mouse will acknowledge the dominant male and stop fighting. Although outsiders to a community generally avoid unknown mice, on occasion an "alien" mouse will come into contact with the mice and a fight ensues.

Mice will use their body parts to intimidate each other, ruffling up their fur to appear larger, slapping their tails and stomping their feet. Mice will bite, wrestle and scratch. These actions, however, can be the same

43

behaviors that females and males will engage in before mating.

CANNIBALISM

Cannibalism has been known to occur when the population of mice is too great for the area to support them. In captivity, overcrowded cages or a scarcity of food can result in cannibalism. If a mother mouse senses that her babies are not healthy, she may eat them.

COPROPHAGY

Coprophagy is another word for eating feces. You may be very unsettled and surprised to discover your own mouse eating his feces, but mice do this in order to get the greatest amount of nutrition from their food. The grass and plants that mice eat are made up of a polysaccharide called cellulose. Cellulose is very difficult to digest. Some animals, such as cows, have an extra stomach chamber in their body with tiny microorganisms that break down the cellulose. Cows can regurgitate partially digested material and chew it a second time. Mice, however, are unable to vomit and must allow food to pass through their body totally before consuming it again.

The body of a mouse contains bacteria, and when food passes through the first time, the stool is coated with vitamin B_1, a valuable vitamin produced by these bacteria. Mice then consume this stool, which travels through the body a second time. This second pass allows the mouse to get extra nutrition from the hard-to-digest plant matter. In the wild, mice will eat their stool if nutrients are scarce. Caged mice may engage in this behavior if their own food supplies are inadequate or if they are stressed.

This behavior may seem odd and even disgusting, but many animals, such as guinea pigs and rabbits, do the same thing.

GROOMING

Mice love to groom themselves. Grooming keeps the mouse meticulously clean. The physical act allows the mouse to stretch and primp. Communities of wild mice will groom one another, cleaning under the chin and other places a single mouse can't reach. Scientists believe that social grooming is another way in which mice communicate with one another.

Another function of grooming is to regulate body temperature. Mammals are endothermic (warm-blooded), maintaining a small range of constant internal temperature as the external temperature fluctuates. Endotherms derive heat from their own metabolism.

A mouse will keep himself clean with frequent grooming.

When they are cold, mammals shiver to produce heat. When the temperature increases, most mammals sweat, which cools the animal as the sweat evaporates from the body. Mice and other rodents, however, lack sweat glands and can't produce the sweat that cools them down. When a mouse becomes warm, he reacts by grooming himself, spreading saliva on the body to promote evaporative cooling. A mouse that becomes too warm and cannot cool down quickly enough will die of heat exhaustion.

HIBERNATION

You may be surprised to find that the little mouse will hibernate. A mouse's heart beats up to 500 beats per minute. This fast beat supplies oxygen to the vital organs, but requires a constant source of energy (food) to be maintained. If a mouse goes to sleep and the body continues to work at such a fast rate without receiving more energy, the mouse can starve to death while asleep. To combat this problem, mice enter a resting stage known as torpor when they sleep. Torpor is referred to as hibernation in the winter and estivation in the summer. During hibernation, a mouse's body temperature falls to that of the environment so that the mouse does not have to produce extra heat to stay warm. In the summer, the more sluggish stage prevents the mouse from overheating. Because the body's functions slow down, mice seem startled when awakened, as if they have been hibernating for the entire winter!

HOMING INSTINCT

Mice have an innate desire to be in contact with solid surfaces, especially when they are out hunting—a time of danger. A mouse will press his body against a wall as if to blend into the background to evade detection. This instinct causes most mice to avoid large, open spaces and to move quickly when they are vulnerable. A mouse can find his way back home in a flash if he needs to. After mice establish a home, they learn the surrounding territory by heart. The little mouse moves cautiously at first, tracing and retracing each of the steps he has taken, memorizing the odors and sounds that naturally occur in the area, until he knows where all objects are that surround his home. By memorizing the layout of the space, mice know not only their areas, but also how to get home in a flash if danger approaches. Mice can zip back into their nests, even on the darkest of nights, because they know exactly where their home is.

NEST BUILDING

Constructing a nest is an innate act for mice. Nests serve many functions. They provide shelter to hide and raise young, protection from the watchful gaze of predators and a place to store nice little snacks. Mice are active animals that use up a lot of energy. Their tiny bodies lose heat easily, so they have to protect themselves, especially when living in cool climates. It is this need that prompts the little house mouse to run off with our sofa stuffing, sewing thread and other household items. These items and other materials the mouse picks up in nature, such as grasses and reeds, are used to construct a solid, well-insulated nest. The mouse makes a hole in the center of the nest, where young can be raised in comfort and privacy, protected from the harsh elements and hungry predators. Surrounding a mouse's nest is a small area designated as "home."

A mouse's nest serves as a place to hide as well as to rear young. In captivity, mice like a place to get away from it all.

Scent Marking

When you own mice, you notice a characteristic odor. The scent is present in the urine, and you'll notice it when you're near the mouse's cage. Glands found at the base of the tail, and on the face, feet or abdomen of the mouse release chemicals that create these odors. These scent markings help mice communicate in a number of ways—from social organization to detecting friend or foe. Mice define their territory by urinating on specific areas. The markings help establish the territory, and mice will usually stay within these boarders. Mice also transfer their odors to one another when grooming each other, giving them a scent the different mice recognize and can identify. Sometimes the scent helps the mouse locate his nest. Sometimes the scent tells males and females they are ready to mate. Sometimes the scent tells a mouse he's in an area that is already occupied by a colony of mice. In the wild, a mouse will not enter this colony for fear of being attacked. The new mouse's scent warns the other mice of an intruder.

Caring
for Your

part two

Mouse

chapter 4

Selecting Your Mouse

Now that you have decided to purchase a mouse (or mice), there are a number of decisions to make, such as:

- Where should I buy my mice?
- How many mice do I want?
- What age should my mice be?
- How do I know if the mice I buy are healthy?
- How can I tell if my mice will be easy to tame?
- Do I want boy or girl mice?

After these decisions are made, you must then decide which mouse or mice will be yours.

Where to Purchase Your Mouse

Purchasing mice requires that you be a good study of both mice and humans. Buying mice can be a spur-of-the-moment decision for some people when they find "their" mice. When choosing a mouse, you have many options. Choosing healthy animals is very important, so you have to be as careful in choosing the buyer as you do in deciding which animal to buy. Keep the following questions in mind when you shop for your new pet:

Are the facilities clean and well maintained? Are the cages clean, or is there a disturbing smell in the air? Does the bedding look fresh? Are food containers filled and water bottles properly hung, or are the mice drinking from a contaminated water dish?

By making sure your future pets are well cared for before they come home with you, you are more likely to be purchasing a healthy mouse. Mice are prone to respiratory illness, which can be the result of being kept in dirty facilities or being kept in the same cage as an infected mouse.

Do the animals look active? Are there any other mice in the cage that look sick, are missing fur or are constantly scratching themselves?

Is the breeder or salesperson knowledgeable about mice? Can he answer your questions, or does he seem disinterested in what he's doing? Does he seem excited that you may come to appreciate mice the way he does, or does he treat the mice as if they are nothing more than snake food? One person wants to help you find a good pet, while the other person may only be interested in unloading merchandise. The seller's level of knowledge and interest is an indication of whether the mice have been treated well.

Don't forget that you're the customer, and don't be afraid to ask questions. And don't feel obligated to leave with a mouse in tow, regardless of how much time you've spent in a shop or breeder's facility. You're looking for "your" pet(s) and need assistance in making the right decision.

Examine the amount of space available for the animals. Do the mice have enough room to run around? Have the mice been kept in cramped surroundings, making them more likely to fight? Are they friendly and sociable? Have males and females been housed together? This is very important! If you choose to bring home a female and she is pregnant, you will end up with more mice than you expected!

How have the mice been bred? Someone who is selling the mice should know if they are the product of a mating between unrelated offspring. Negligent breeders may mate littermates or closely related animals (brother and sister, mother and son). This is a bad idea, because it increases the likelihood of hereditary diseases. These problems are usually obvious when you see the mice, but may not show themselves until the mouse is a little older. Hereditary diseases can shorten a mouse's life span and subject the mouse to pain.

Albino mice are the most commonly available variety at stores.

Are you purchasing the mouse for show? If so, remember that some clubs have standards mice need to conform to if they are going to compete and win ribbons. There are shows for mice without "proper" lineage and these shows can be just as fun as the formal shows. Pet mice make great companions whether they are show mice or not, so this question is only relevant if you have a burning desire to exhibit your future pet. If you decide you are interested in fancy mice, you should contact a breeder or attend a show.

PET SHOPS

Pet shops are a good place to shop if you're looking for a companion mouse. They're also a great option for one-stop shopping. You can find accessories to accommodate the cage you have (hopefully) set up ahead of time. A disadvantage to purchasing a mouse in a pet shop is that you are less likely to find mice with interesting colors or patterns, although this is not always the case. Indeed, some smaller stores will carry a larger variety of mice than you'll find in the superstores. As a rule, most of the mice carried by the superstores are albino mice (that are just as lovable as any other kind!).

BREEDERS

You undoubtedly will spend more if you purchase from a breeder than you will if you buy your mouse in a pet shop. The difference may be as much as ten to thirty dollars, but good breeders try to provide quality animals. They breed mice specifically to be hardy and tame. These breeders may also offer mice in the varieties that are very difficult to come by in pet shops, such as English mice, Siamese and Rexes.

If you're looking for a "designer" pet, such as this longhaired mouse, you may have to buy from a breeder.

Unfortunately, breeders can be difficult to locate. You might try searching the Yellow Pages, but a better source would probably be your local fancy mouse association. A number of them are listed at the back of this book. Check the Internet for breeders by searching the heading "fancy mice." Small pet magazines also provide breeder contacts in the advertisements at the back.

Be prepared to be "grilled" a bit when you first contact a breeder. Some people will contact breeders looking for mice to use as food for their pets, and some breeders choose not to sell mice for this purpose. When you make clear that you are interested in mice as pets, you will almost always get a breeder's cooperation. A good breeder will appreciate your interest and delight in mice.

CLUBS AND SHOWS

Attending local mouse and pet shows can be a great way to meet people with similar interests while checking out the mice of some local breeders. Breeding mice has become a popular hobby for people of all ages. Meeting breeders at clubs and shows gives you access to a wide variety of mice and is a great way to learn about your new pet. A word of caution however: Be sure you set up a cage before you attend, because you may find your mice waiting for you at the show!

ANIMAL SHELTERS AND OTHER OPTIONS

Other options you have for acquiring a mouse include contacting a local animal shelter or veterinarian's office. Many shelters will adopt out unwanted mice, as well as dogs and cats. Some owners will post notices at their veterinary clinic if they are unable to keep their pet. When you adopt a pet from either source, you're giving an unwanted animal a good home. Some clinics will allow you to post a "Mice Wanted" ad at their facility so that people can contact you if they have a mouse.

How Many Mice?

Wild mice live in communities and are sociable creatures. They rely on one another for warmth and companionship. Mice attend to one another's needs. They enjoy grooming one another, playing with each other and cuddling together. When deciding how many mice to purchase, buy at least two if you can. Despite information to the contrary, keeping multiple mice will not limit their attachment to you. Even if they have one another for companionship, your mice will befriend you, too! Just be sure to let them get to know you.

Mice that live alone are often bored and isolated, especially if you do not have enough time to give to them each and every day. Single mice may engage in self-mutilating activities because they are so lonely. If you are able to keep only one mouse, spend at least an hour a day with her. She will be relying on you for all the physical and social interaction she would naturally receive in a colony.

Male or Female

Male and female mice require the same amount of care and handling. If you choose to buy male mice, be aware that they produce a stronger, muskier odor than

In a male mouse, the testicles are apparent.

their female counterparts. Cleaning the cage properly and consistently will prevent much of this problem. Broadly, a group or pair of females will get along better than a group or pair of males. Adult males may fight, especially if they are introduced when grown. If they are raised together from a young age (about 5 to 6 weeks of age) and are from the same litter, they tend to get along. Make sure that you do not choose a male and a female, otherwise you will have more mice than you expect. Mice are prolific breeders! If you discover you have chosen a male and female once you get your mice home, do not keep them in the same cage.

HOW TO DETERMINE THE SEX
OF A MOUSE

*In a female
mouse, the geni-
tals are set close
to the anus.*

It's much easier to determine the sex of older mice
than it is younger mice. Adult males are generally
larger than adult females. In adult mice, the distance
between the anus and the genitals is closer in females
and farther apart in males. The scrotum, in males, is
located at the base of the tail and the testicles are obvious, even when the male is sitting. Determining the sex
in younger mice is more
difficult. Only female mice
have nipples, which are
noticeable after 10 days of
age. The nipples run
down the length of the
body in five pairs. By running your finger along the
belly, you should be able
to find them if you feel
closely.

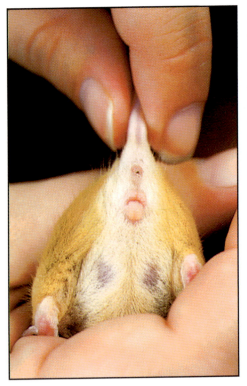

Age

You want to buy a young
mouse. Mice have a short
life span, ordinarily living
fewer than three years.
Mice have been reported
to live as long as seven
years, but this is an
uncommon occurrence,
even with the best of care.
Younger mice are also
easier to tame. You can usually distinguish a young
mouse from an adult mouse by her smaller size and
shinier, fuzzy coat. Younger mice may have more hair
on their tails. Mice are weaned at 4 weeks of age and
are ideally purchased when they are 5 or 6 weeks
old. Ask the person helping you how old the mice are
and to point out mice of different ages so that you can
compare them.

Evaluating Health

As mice are short-lived, you'll be able to enjoy your mouse longer if you buy one that is young and healthy. You want to choose a mouse with a glossy coat, bright eyes and a clean nose, mouth and anus. The mouse should be breathing normally. She should not have any sores, scabs or bald patches, all of which can be signs of illness or parasites. Mice should be lean, neither too fat nor too thin, and have no signs of lameness. Healthy mice are alert, busy and curious when you approach.

Symptoms of unhealthy mice include constant or intermittent sneezing, wheezing or rattled breathing; dull, half-open or runny eyes; runny nose; and fur that is not well kept. Fur stained by diarrhea signals disease, as does lethargy. A hunched back can be symptomatic of an ill or an elderly mouse. Sometimes mice will start sneezing when their bedding is changed, so inquire about when this last occurred if you see the mice sneezing. Mice should not be chewed on by other mice, which can indicate a situation of barbering or aggression (described in chapter 8). All body parts should be in good shape. Missing or duplicate limbs are obvious signs of genetic disorders.

Watch all the mice for a good period of time. Each mouse in the cage should be well. If any one of the mice shows symptoms of illness or infestation, all mice have probably been exposed to the problem. A mouse taken from these surroundings will require much more maintenance than a healthy mouse.

Evaluating Temperament

The best pet is both healthy and well socialized. When you approach the cage, pay attention to which mice are interested in your scent. Do they want to get a better sniff of you? When the cage is opened, do they scurry into the corner and try to hide, or do they stand up on their hind legs and attempt to smell you? Socialized mice are curious about you. They may be nervous at first, because mice are generally timid animals, but will soon assess the situation and approach you. Any mouse that makes an effort to investigate you is likely to make a great pet. Mice that have not been handled often are unsure and skittish. These mice are more difficult to tame and require greater time and effort.

Once you have permission to reach into the cage, see if any of the mice will allow you to pick them up. Reject any mouse that tries to bite. Mice do not bite unless they are frightened, but a scared mouse is one that is not well tamed. This is an especially poor pet for a child. A mouse that squeaks or attempts to run away is saying to you that she is not the best choice. A better choice is the mouse that approaches you and is interested in seeing what you have to offer. When holding a mouse, be sure to keep your hands in a cupped position to protect her from falling. An interested mouse will sniff at you to see if you are a good match for her!

If you are looking at mice in different cages, wash your hands before touching mice in a second cage. This helps prevent the spread of disease.

It's so exciting when your new friend comes home!

You may just fall in love with a mouse because of her special appearance, even if she's not as friendly as she could be. If you must give in to your whim, recognize that there will be more work involved in socializing this new friend. Take her home if you're confident that you'll have the time to devote to taming her.

Bringing Your New Friend Home

Once you've chosen your new friend(s) and are ready to go home, make sure the pet carrier is secure. (This can be a smaller cage you will keep on hand or the cardboard box the seller gives you.) On the ride home, resist the urge to open the box and peer at your new pets. Let your mice relax and do not attempt to take them out. They will be nervous about the car ride and may try to escape. Wait until you get home to inspect your new friend(s).

THE FIRST DAY

On your new pets' first day home, be sure you have all the supplies set up properly. Leave the nest box out of the cage until you've spent some time taming your mice. This will prevent them from hiding and resisting meeting you. Let your mice out into their new home and allow them time to get acclimated. They will want to sniff the new shavings, choose a spot to make nests and generally get acquainted with their new surroundings.

Moving is scary! Have the cage and accessories ready for your mouse.

Observe them as they settle in. Give them at least four hours alone without disturbing them before you introduce yourself—give them the whole day if you can control yourself. Moving is quite traumatic and stressful (just like it is for people!). Some quiet time will give them an opportunity to adjust.

Move quietly and slowly when you do approach for the first time. Gauge your introduction to your pets' reaction. For example, a mouse that quickly retreats to a corner and stays frozen or runs around rapidly is not ready to meet you. Give her the time to acclimate. Mice that stand up and sniff when the lid is removed may be ready to say hello.

You may place your hand in the cage, but make no attempt to touch the mice. Avoid making sudden movements. Let the mice get used to your scent. Hold a treat between your fingers to encourage them to explore your hand. They will probably walk right onto your palm to retrieve the treat. But this may not occur until you and your mice are better acquainted. Try not to hold the mice for the first day, just allow them to get used to the sudden change in surroundings and the new scents. A mouse may try to escape before she gets to know you, so be sure that all cage doors are closed tightly. A scared mouse can jump right out of the cage and run away! By giving your new pets time to settle in, you are investing in an easier transition for them. Your patience will be rewarded in the long run.

Handling Your Mouse

After your mouse has had a day or two to get used to her new surroundings, let your pet know you're going to be good friends. It will take some time for your new pal to recognize your scent as a friendly one. Until that time comes, use care when handling these small creatures. Mice are sturdy animals, but some body parts can be fragile. There are different opinions as to how to pick up a mouse. The entire body must be held because the little mouse is so tiny that she can be crushed if she's squeezed or stepped on.

Never grab a mouse at the tip of her tail. This area is very tender and delicate and can break off easily. This is especially true in younger mice. It is generally agreed that picking a mouse up by the base of her tail is not cruel, but it is not the preferred method

KEEP TO A SCHEDULE

Mice like routine. Make an effort to play with your mouse and care for her surroundings at the same time each day. By cleaning out the cage before playing with her, you give the mouse an opportunity to become aware of your presence, especially if she's been napping. After you've refreshed her supplies, take out your friend and spend some quality time together. It is best to spend at least thirty minutes a day with multiple mice, one hour if you have only one mouse. You will soon notice that your mouse is already waiting for you and her "play-date."

either. If you do choose to pick up your mouse this way, do not dangle the mouse in the air, but instead quickly slip your hand under the mouse's belly for support. If the mouse is particularly skittish, keep a grip on the base of the tail until you are satisfied that the mouse has gotten used to you. Most mice will not jump from heights, but a nervous mouse may do anything to get away.

A better method is to slide one hand under the mouse and gently cup the other hand over the top of the mouse's body to ease her out of the cage. Another option for mice that are not fully tamed is to take a small cup or a toilet paper roll, scoop the mouse up and then gently drop her into your hands. Once your animal becomes tame, she should walk right into your hands because she knows it is time to play. Cupping your hands together is a great way to carry your mouse. Mice like to explore and will slip in and out of your sleeves and pockets. Mice will generally not jump from your hands, but they do love to climb. A quick mouse may try to use you as a ladder, climbing down to the ground and off to who knows where! Some mice will be just as content to investigate you or to groom themselves while you admire them.

The Escape Artist

Mice are inquisitive by nature, so it is never wise to let a mouse run around by herself. Wild mice are timid and uninterested in human contact. Pet mice are bred to be more confident, but even a pet mouse will be increasingly difficult to train if she is allowed to run and hide from you. Don't forget that a mouse can adapt to most surroundings and could live her whole life in your home without returning to the cage. Remember that mice are curious and will want to explore their surroundings. Moreover, because of their small size, they can easily hide.

An escaped mouse can be difficult to catch, especially if she hasn't been tamed. If your mouse does escape, try to trap her in one room where you can easily retrieve her. The living room and kitchen are not ideal places. Little runaways may choose to hide behind an extremely heavy bookcase or refrigerator. Successfully retrieving the pet will require more work in reestablishing a relationship after the mouse has had a taste of freedom. After such an experience, the mouse may still try to escape again.

To prevent a mouse's escape, don't put the mouse directly on the open floor. If you do want to put the mouse down on something and interact, a bed is a good choice because you can scoop her right up. Tables are best if the edge extends over the leg. Mice will generally not jump from such a height and will not be able to scurry down the table leg if the top extends beyond the leg. This is fun for you as well, because you can set up some toys and watch your mice play.

Once a mouse escapes, there's no end to the trouble she may get herself into.

Mice and Other Pets

Most house pets are natural predators of the mouse, including ferrets, reptiles and other rodents. Some dogs were bred specifically to hunt mice, and cats are known for their interest in capturing mice. When bringing mice into a home where other pets already reside, take the time to introduce pets properly. It is best for mice to stay separated from these other pets that would love to make a delicious meal of your little pet. This means not only refraining from playing with them in the same room, but keeping them in different parts of the home as well.

Rats and mice should not be kept together. The larger rat can injure the smaller mouse. Rats can also be carriers of bacteria that are not harmful to them but cause blood poisoning in mice. Some rat owners do report success in keeping mice and rats together, but this is not generally recommended.

IF YOU HAVE A CAT OR DOG

In a *few* instances, it is possible for some dogs and cats to get along with mice, especially if they are introduced when they are puppies and kittens. Don't think that you can fool your dog or cat—with their keen sense of smell these animals will definitely know there is someone new in their house. The dog or cat will want to sniff the mouse. Mice should remain in the cage while the dog or cat observes them. Cats and dogs will react differently, depending on their personalities. Some dogs will bark while others will stand at attention. Some cats will stare transfixed at the cage and others will walk by without a second glance.

Teaching the dog or cat to accept the mouse can be a real challenge. If you bring the mouse out for an introduction, have someone else hold the dog or cat while you hold the mouse. Watch for signs of aggression, such as snapping or stalking. In most cases, mice are simply too vulnerable to the instincts of other pets and must remain in the cage when other animals are around.

What About Me?

Believe it or not, your dog or cat can become jealous of a little mouse! They see this other pet coming into the home, watch you interact with her and think there won't be enough attention for them. You may notice your dog butting its head against you every time you head for the cage. Your cat may meow loudly and crawl between your legs, tripping you, while you try to feed the mouse. These pets are saying, "What about me?"

To help ease anxiety of being upstaged, try petting your dog or talking to your cat as you sit in front of the cage. You want your dog or cat to associate the mouse with more attention for them. This can help them be more accepting of your newest addition.

63

chapter 5

Housing
Your
Mouse

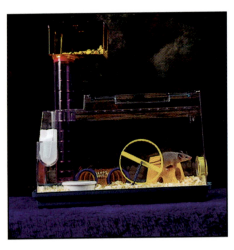

In the wild, a colony of mice would establish a small, secure area and use the surrounding territory for food and recreation. Mice are curious creatures and love to explore. This constant activity keeps them healthy. Your mouse should have the same advantages of space, safety and activity in a cage.

The most important thing to remember when deciding on a cage is that you want this to be a home for your pet, not a prison. The cage must provide adequate space for your mouse and allow you to easily remove the mouse and clean the cage, yet be sturdy enough to protect your mouse from predators and small children.

Cages are available in all shapes, sizes and prices. These enclosures should be roomy so that the mice can move about freely and should be large enough to accommodate toys and accessories. Mice will define areas in which they eat, sleep, play and eliminate waste.

These creatures prefer to eliminate in a corner as far as possible from where they eat and sleep. Suitable space is thus a requirement not only of comfort, but of proper hygiene.

A cage must also be well built so that it is easy for you to clean. Proper husbandry is the best way to keep your animal healthy. Keep in mind that you want to be able to get your mouse out of the cage easily, with as little stress to the mouse as possible. You want to be able to get the lid off easily, but not have it come off so easily that a dog, cat or unsupervised child could release the mouse.

> ### VERTICAL CAGES
>
> If you don't have room for a cage that takes up counter space, consider purchasing or constructing one that climbs upward. This option can give mice the activity and freedom they enjoy. A cage with different layers and platforms, attached by ropes and ladders, gives mice an instant playground as well as a home. It also gives you another opportunity to see them in action. Although you may have a hard time finding a vertical cage, check your local pet supply shops and superstores. If constructing a vertical cage yourself, avoid using cardboard and wood.

A cage that is too heavy or too bulky is difficult to clean. Your best choice is a cage that is easy to take apart and to reassemble. Good construction is important so the mice do not catch their tiny feet in corners or cracks. This is especially true in cages with wire or mesh floors.

Types of Cages

MAKING YOUR OWN

Some people like to build their own cages. If you do, be sure to keep in mind the caging essentials noted above. There are a number of books to help you if you are interested in making a home for your mouse yourself. Most such manuals are directed toward constructing a home for hamsters and rats, but they can be useful in helping to build a mouse's cage if you keep the mouse's smaller size in mind.

WIRE CAGES

Wire cages can be a great choice, especially if there are no other pets in the household. These cages allow air to circulate easily and thereby help to provide a healthy environment. Mice can enjoy themselves climbing across the wires and can easily smell the scents in the air. Many wire cages are specially coated to prevent rust. Attaching toys, dishes and water bottles to the sides of the cage gives your mouse more room for playing.

Wire cages provide lots of air circulation—just be sure that your mouse can't get out!

However, there are drawbacks to wire cages. You must make sure that the mouse cannot squeeze between the wires. There should be no more than ¼ inch between the bars. Another drawback to wire cages is that mice can kick the bedding out of the cage. Unsightly "spillage" can be controlled by putting the cage in a pan with sides high enough to capture the lost bedding. Some cages are built with a panel lining in the bottom that will aid in keeping the bedding inside.

With a wire cage, you have to take extra caution so the wires can't be used as leverage to bring the cage down. As examples, a cat can use its paw, or a small child can use her fingers to drag the cage from its resting place. When a mouse is clinging to the wires, don't yank him off, as this can injure your pet. Wait until he's climbed down and scoop him into a cup. Wire cages can rust if they are not specially treated, so be sure to dry them thoroughly after they are washed.

GLASS CAGES

Aquariums are another great way to house your pet. A 10-gallon aquarium works well for two to four mice. You can usually purchase aquariums with a wire cover, or get one to fit at the local hardware store. Aquariums are durable; they protect mice from drafts; bedding is contained; and mice are able to burrow without making a mess. With a removable lid, you have instant access to all corners of the cage, and you can easily rearrange toys to make the home more interesting.

On the downside, glass cages are difficult to clean. Aquariums are bulky and heavy, so lifting one (even without water in it) is not easy. Moreover, if the glass cracks, it can ultimately chip, and glass chips are obviously *not* something that you want your mouse to ingest. Because they are heavy and breakable, aquariums are usually not a good housing choice if a younger child is responsible for the mouse.

Glass cages are attractive homes, but they can become very hot. Don't place a glass cage in direct sunlight.

Another drawback is the lack of air circulation in a solid glass cage. If the air becomes stale, bacteria may build up in the cage, leading to respiratory illness in your pet. A mouse kept in a glass cage is also more susceptible to heatstroke than a mouse that lives in an airier home. To keep the cage from becoming too hot, a mouse's cage should never be set in direct sunlight. This rule applies no matter what type of cage you select, but is especially important if you choose a glass enclosure.

For glass cages, meticulous cleaning is imperative. The slick sides of the aquarium should prevent the mice from escaping, but be sure that no toys provide access to the lid and that the lid is secure.

PLASTIC CAGES

Modern durable plastics are an excellent way to house a mouse. These cages are produced by many manufacturers of pet supplies. They are lightweight, so they are easy to lift and to clean. They're also easy to carry if you want to take your mouse with you. Many come equipped with wheels, tunnels and nesting boxes attached, so you can provide fewer toys and the mice can get plenty of exercise. Watching your pets enjoy this type of cage can also be fun for you.

A drawback to a plastic cage is poor ventilation. Newer models will often have small holes drilled at the top of the cage to increase ventilation, but you can drill these yourself if they aren't already present. Other plastic cages offer an attachment with holes so that the cage gets cross ventilation. Be aware that the attachments can wear down with time and can be difficult to reassemble when dismantled for cleaning. Because proper hygiene is so important to the mouse's life, replace these items when they wear down.

CAGE MATERIALS TO AVOID

Cardboard and wooden boxes are not ideal for housing a mouse. They are fine if you need to hold mice for a brief period of time or to transport them, but not for long-term accommodations. Urine saturates cardboard, making it smell and crumble. Mice love to gnaw and can easily make a hole in the wood or cardboard, creating an exit for themselves. Wood and cardboard can be used as accessories, but will need to be replaced often. Wire cages or durable plastic cages and glass aquariums make much better homes.

A WORD ABOUT LIDS AND LOCKS

Keeping the little mouse protected within the cage is an important aspect in caring for your pet. Plastic cages usually come with self-locking lids that prevent the mouse from escaping. Sometimes a resourceful mouse will scoot his way up to the top of the wheel and squeeze out through the thin lid. Your best defense is to choose a cover that seals tightly or to use locks to prevent such clever attempts. Glass aquariums usually require you to purchase a screen cover that provides air and prevents escape. There are various types of screens on the market. Just make sure that you can lock the lid in place—you can purchase a cage lock that attaches to the glass. You can also purchase a self-locking cage cover. New designs include security suction cups that attach to the lid and to the side of the cage. Other locks are clips that twist into place and stay secured against the glass. A good pet shop will offer a variety of these items.

Where to Put the Cage

Not only is the structure of the cage important, but where you place your mouse's home must also be considered. Dangers can exist everywhere for your tiny pet despite a solid cage. Mice are susceptible to direct sunlight, drafts or the paw of a clever cat.

Placing a cage on a countertop or desk is a good choice. It protects the mouse from humidity and drafts, places him where you can watch him and he can see you, and puts him in the center of activity. You can enjoy your mouse more easily because you can watch him play. A cage that sits on the floor is likely to be ignored.

> **HAVE A HOME READY FOR YOUR MOUSE**
>
> Before you bring your mouse home, do a little pre-pet shopping. Be sure to have:
>
> Cage with a cover and lock
>
> Bedding
>
> Food
>
> Food dish
>
> Water bottle
>
> Nest box and nesting materials
>
> Toys

Mice also need to be placed in a partially lit room with plenty of fresh air and away from direct sunlight. Most mammals sweat to release heat and cool their bodies, but rodents lack sweat glands. As a result, mice are very sensitive to heat. They do best at about 68°F (20°C), which is usually considered average room temperature. A temperature close to or above 88°F (30°C) can

69

cause heatstroke and death. Don't forget that aquariums and plastic cages heat up easily. The temperature inside the cage is greater than outside the cage, and direct sunlight can become deadly. Be sure not to place the cage on a windowsill or under a vent. A draft can make your mouse uncomfortable or ill.

Bedding

Mice love to burrow and create a den. Bedding gives mice this nesting material, keeps a cage dry and comfortable and protects little paws. Bedding materials must be highly absorbent and must be changed often. Mice have fastidious grooming habits, but they are still susceptible to bacteria that will germinate in unsanitary conditions. Their urine has a distinct odor, so change bedding at least once a week to eliminate this problem. You may need to change bedding more often, depending on the number of mice you have. To minimize odor, place a little cat litter or baking soda in the corners of the cage where the mice are most likely to urinate. The litter or baking soda needs to be replaced when you change the bedding and is in no way an adequate substitute for proper housekeeping.

TYPES OF BEDDING

There is a great variety of bedding products on the market. Wood shavings, such as pine and cedar shavings (described below), are the most common types of bedding found. However, newly introduced products are competing with the more common forms of bedding. The more recent introductions to the market include citrus litter, grass fiber pellets, aspen or oak bedding, alfalfa pellets, corncob products and recycled paper products. Many of these products are popular because they are dust-free, reducing irritation to the mouse's respiratory system. They also control odor and recycle natural resources. Whereas regular newsprint contains chemicals that are toxic to your mice, recycled newspaper is acceptable. The recycling process eliminates the harmful chemicals.

Pine and cedar shavings are popular due to their wide availability and low cost. Pine shavings are available in green (colored with chlorophyll) and white (plain pinewood), whereas cedar shavings are found in a variety of colors, including red and white.

Regardless of the type of bedding you choose, it must be completely replaced at least once a week.

These shavings also contain chemicals that kill parasites, such as mites. However, this same chemical makeup has made this bedding choice controversial in the last few years. Some studies report that the phenols in pine and cedar shavings are the problem. Phenols are poisonous compounds used to disguise odors, and they give pine and cedar the nice smell that masks a mousy aroma. But phenols are also suspected of irritating the animals' skin and respiratory system, making mice vulnerable to pneumonia, and of doing damage to the liver and kidneys, key organs in maintaining health.

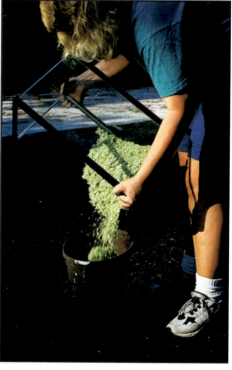

The liver and kidneys are the body's filters, processing contaminants out of the body. In large quantities, these toxins can build up in the body's system, preventing the liver and kidneys from functioning properly and severely limiting the mouse's already short life span. Cedar shavings are believed to be more caustic than pine shavings. Check with your breeder, pet supplier and/or veterinarian if you have concerns about this kind of bedding.

CHOOSE BEDDING WITH CARE

Even a product as uncomplicated as bedding can pose health risks to your mouse. Bedding may look and

71

smell fine to you, but microorganisms and chemical treatments can expose your pet to illness. Your best defense is to purchase processed bedding sold in pet supply shops and superstores. These products have been specifically manufactured with small animal needs in mind. When you purchase bedding (or hay or alfalfa) from local stables and sawmills, you run the risk of giving your mice materials contaminated by wild mice. Even minute amounts of urine and droppings from wild mice can transfer disease to your otherwise healthy pet. Bedding must be dry and dust-free to reduce irritation to the mouse's respiratory system. If you notice symptoms such as rattled breathing, sneezing or secretions around the eyes and nose, you may be witnessing a respiratory illness associated with the use of bedding that is harmful to your pet. When choosing bedding, buy small amounts at first and decide what works best for you and your pets.

Nest Box and Nesting Materials

Because mice nest instinctively, they will be most comfortable if you give them something they can turn into a nest box. This can be purchased at the pet shop or created in your own home, a fun activity for smaller children. If you use a cardboard or wooden box (which must be cleaned and replaced often), avoid using products such as glue and staples, which would be harmful to the mouse if ingested. Make sure all products are labeled nontoxic to pets.

SIZE DOES MATTER!

If you've ever lived in a studio apartment, you know how important a little legroom can be. Whether you choose a wire, plastic or aquarium cage, think about the size of your new friend's home. The cage should be at least $10 \times 10 \times 15$ inches if you're keeping two or three mice (or a 10-gallon aquarium) with no more than $\frac{1}{4}$-inch between the wires if you are using a wire cage.

All that is required of the box is to provide a sleeping or hiding space with an entrance/exit and holes for ventilation. The box must be made of nontoxic materials because the mouse will gnaw at it. It is acceptable to use the regular bedding in the nest box, but for something different you may want to give your mouse hay or alfalfa from the local pet shop. These alternatives give the cage a fresh scent and give the mouse something different to chew on. Fabrics and paper towels can be used as well. Just be sure that what you are giving your pet doesn't have any harmful chemicals. Part of the fun of a nest box is watching mice drag different items into the box as they create their personal space.

Cage Accessories
FOOD DISHES

Food dishes should be sturdy and durable. Mice will chew dishes made of soft plastic. You want to be sure that the mouse cannot tip the dish over and spill the food. Ceramic dishes are popular for this reason. They are sturdy and easy to clean. If space permits, you may want to have a second bowl for different types of treats, such as fruits or vegetables. Hard plastic dishes that attach to the sides of the cage are also a good option.

A clean, full and functional water bottle is a must.

WATER BOTTLES

It is vital to your mouse's well-being that he have access to fresh water. For this reason, it is very important to choose a reliable water bottle that functions properly, regardless of the cost. Suspended water bottles are better than dishes, which can accumulate bedding and droppings, as well as tip over and saturate the cage. Once the water dish has spilled, the bedding becomes a haven for unwanted bacteria. There are

various types of bottles. Your choice will depend in part on the cage you choose. Wire cages allow the bottle to be attached directly to the side of the cage, whereas durable plastic or aquarium cages use a metal wand to hang the water bottle into the cage. If you have an aquarium or durable plastic cage, make sure the bottle extends deep enough for the mouse to reach it.

A good water bottle will provide your mouse with plenty of water whenever he wants it, but will neither withhold water nor leak all over the cage. Glass bottles with rubber stoppers can work well. They create a good seal, so they dispense water only on demand. Some mice, however, cannot resist chewing on the rubber stopper, causing the water to leak out. If the glass breaks from the mouse's gnawing, it can injure the mouse. A second option is a plastic water bottle with a metal ball at the tip. This offers the same demand-type action as the glass bottle, but is less likely to leak. On occasion, you may find that a plastic bottle will not release the water at all. No matter what type of bottle you choose, be sure to check it every day for leaks and access. You can check availability by pressing your finger against the end of the tube. Water should come out in small amounts and create a fair-sized drop. Be sure your mice are not pushing bedding around the bottle or into the tube source, cutting off access to water themselves.

A mouse will enjoy exploring his toys.

Toys

Toys are an important component in raising a healthy mouse. Along with good nutrition and fresh water, physical activity keeps a mouse trim and happy. Without toys, mice will gnaw at their cage, food dish or water bottle. Toys help limit self-traumatizing behavior and give mice an outlet for the excess energy that is part of their natural character. Mice love to climb, hide, explore and burrow.

Mice work hard and will put their toys to good use. Products may be purchased or made with the tiny gnawer in mind. Toys made of soft plastic will disappear quickly and are not a good choice. Consider spending a few extra dollars on the more expensive toys and accessories if they move more easily or are more durable. It is true that a little expense here and there will add up, but it is wiser to spend a little more initially than it is to purchase an item that doesn't work properly or is chewed up immediately.

To keep playtime interesting, rearrange and exchange toys on occasion. Replace worn-out items and anything with sharp edges. Do not put too many items in the cage at once, however, for this can clutter the cage and prevent the mice from running freely. Watching your mice play in this environment is not only good for their health, but for yours as well!

A cautionary note about toys—avoid placing items from outdoors in your mouse's cage. Sticks and the like may have been treated with pesticides and may contain microscopic parasites.

EXERCISE WHEEL

Exercise wheels are one of the most common forms of entertainment for mice. Some cages come with a wheel installed while others do not. If you have a cage that is not equipped with a wheel, be sure to buy one. Before purchasing the wheel, check to see that it spins properly without requiring too much effort. The

Thank goodness man invented the wheel!

wheel must also fit the cage, taking up no more than one-quarter to one-third of the cage space, still allowing your pet plenty of room to move about. Mice love using their wheel and will run for quite a while. Be aware that although awake during day and night, mice are more likely to be active during the very early hours of the day (such as 3 a.m.) and will want to run on the wheel. You may decide to keep the mice in another room so that you can sleep and they can exercise without either of you disturbing the other.

A small exercise ball will allow your mouse to work out in safety.

EXERCISE BALL

Another common item for mice is a plastic exercise ball with a locking top. The ball encases the mouse so that he can run on the ground, yet remain protected from feet and other pets. The balls are most often purchased for gerbils and hamsters, but some can be used for adult mice. Look for products designed with mice in mind. The tiny feet of younger mice can become trapped in the air slits, so be very cautious if your mouse is not yet an adult. Always observe your mouse when he's out and about in his ball, especially if other pets are nearby. Make sure the plastic ball does not sit in direct sunlight or that the ball is not used near stairs. Keep in mind that this is a place for temporary play and not a place to keep the mouse for long periods of time.

OTHER TOYS

Pet stores carry a variety of toys for rodents, from little boots and cabins and houses made of plastic and wood to wooden chew toys and complete play kits designed to entertain your pet. We love our pets and we want to spoil them. As a result, the pet industry has created an overwhelming array of fun and interesting options for mice. Something as basic as extra tubing that connects the home cage to a smaller one gives the mice plenty to do. New cage tops now incorporate accessories, such as extra wheels, tunnels and towers!

Hard rubber bones are another option—these give your mouse something to really chew on. Some products designed for small birds also can be used for mice, such as ladders or ropes to stretch across the cage. New products that enrich little lives are developed every day! Pet magazines feature the latest toys and products for your small friend. If you can't find the toy you want when out shopping, check the advertisements in pet care magazines. You'll often be able to order the toy or obtain a catalog from the manufacturer.

Not all toys have to be purchased. Mice can get hours of fun from toilet paper rolls and paper towel rolls. They shred these up and add them to their bedding, as well as hiding within them and peering out at you. Small boxes also work well. Other items that you find around your home can be incorporated with caution. Shipping materials often contain chemicals harmful to pets, as do some processed materials. As stated earlier, wood and cardboard will absorb urine, so replace them often. Mice love to run up ropes and ladders; attaching one to the top of the cage gives mice another fun way to work out. Just be sure you are not giving them a way out of the cage!

Extra Cages

Having an extra, smaller cage on hand is always a good idea. With multiple mice in a household, you may need to separate an aggressive or ill mouse. The smaller cage is a good place to put your mouse when you are cleaning out his larger home. If you have limited space when traveling and need to disassemble the larger cage until you arrive at your location, the mouse can travel easily in the smaller cage.

Cleaning the Cage

Keeping your mouse's cage clean and secure is a must if you want to provide a healthy environment. With proper care every day, the likelihood of disease is dramatically decreased. Daily responsibilities include

emptying and replenishing the food dish. Look for uneaten or wilted food or debris and remove it. This must be done every day to limit bacterial growth. Change the water every day so you're sure it's fresh. Check for leaks so bedding remains dry and so your mice have constant access to water.

Replace bedding at least once a week, but a twice-weekly cleaning is better. One mouse alone can have over thirty droppings a day, not to mention urine. The number of mice you keep and the amount of mess they

After cleaning, rinse the cage thoroughly.

make will help you determine whether or not the cage needs a biweekly cleaning. If you have two or more animals and ventilation is poor, increased cleaning is a must. If proper hygiene is overlooked or unattended, it creates a health risk for your pet.

Weekly responsibilities include an overall cleaning of the cage. Everything must be removed and cleaned with soap and hot water. Scrub thoroughly, including corners and between the bars. This includes all toys and accessories. Avoid using harsh cleansers as they usually contain chemicals that can be harmful to mice. Grocery and pet stores may have pet-safe cleaning supplies, but a mild soap is fine. Be sure to rinse everything completely so that no soap residue remains and to dry the cage and accessories thoroughly.

chapter 6

Feeding Your Mouse

Good nutrition is one of the most important aspects of keeping your mouse healthy. A poor diet may be the result of picky eating habits on the mouse's part—she may choose to eat only fattier portions of the offered diet. It may also occur when there is no clear feeding schedule and the mouse must rely on treats.

Feeding your mouse properly is not at all difficult. Mice are omnivores, which means they eat both plant and animal products. Mice are always interested in trying something new. After all, these are the same creatures that will feast on soap and leather!

The Staple Diet

PELLETS

Commercial diets have been formulated for mice. This food comes in the form of pellets, which are powdered mixtures compressed into a block form that provide the appropriate concentrations of required vitamins, minerals and trace elements. In addition to being nutritious, pellets are hard and will do a good job of wearing down your mouse's teeth. You can usually purchase the pellets at pet shops and superstores, or you may be able to buy them from your veterinarian. Using commercial diets is an easy way to feed your mouse and you can supplement with fresh foods and treats. Pellets are the food of choice for laboratories—they are easy to feed and the mice find them tasty.

By giving your mouse pellets as the basis of her diet and supplementing them with smaller helpings of other foods, she will receive a nutritious diet. Tasty alternatives also keep the diet from being boring and bland. Pellets, or lab blocks as they are sometimes called, should be available at all times, unless you have an obese mouse. Because bulk foods can become stale quickly, buy smaller amounts and keep them in air-tight containers to guarantee freshness and durability.

GOOD MOUSE FOOD

Mouse pellets

Fruits and vegetables

Seeds and grains

Unseasoned cooked meats and legumes

NOT TOO MUCH OR WE'LL GET FAT

Sunflower seeds

Bacon

Eggs

Cheese

NONE FOR US, THANK YOU

Candy

Chips

Soda

Whatever you know in your heart is junk food

SEEDS

Seed diets for mice are also available in pet stores. Just like we all go for the cashews in a can of mixed nuts, mice will often pick out the better-tasting seeds, which are usually high in fat and low in nutrition. A common ingredient is the sunflower seed, which mice love, but is better as a treat than a typical meal. Some people recommend mixing the pellets with the seed diets, but mice will avoid the pellets and feast on the fattier, less nutritious seeds.

Pellets designed for mice are a good staple food.

Healthy Supplements

Mice have a high metabolic rate and will eat small meals throughout the day. While the pellets you offer are nutritious and tasty, mice need variety. Wild mice have plenty of options, and you can provide that variety to your domesticated pal. Healthy supplements include fruits, vegetables, grains, seeds, meats and protein. Remove uneaten food in a timely manner so that there is no rotting.

These foods should be given in small amounts once a day, depending upon the chosen food. Always introduce new foods in tiny amounts to prevent stomach upset and diarrhea. Do not provide too many options or provide the food so often that mice come to rely on these supplements as their sole source of nutrition and ignore the pellets. Pet stores sell a variety of treats made from wheat and sugar or yogurt. These should be given as a small supplement only, perhaps once a week, and should never be substituted for the pellets. Not all treats have to be purchased. Your own home has a variety of edible delights!

81

FRUITS AND VEGETABLES

Fruits and vegetables are important to mice. Mice enjoy gnawing on many raw vegetables and nibbling on fresh fruit. Examine fresh fruit and vegetables closely to make sure that they are not wilted or rotten. Green vegetables and citrus fruits can cause diarrhea, so give these in moderate amounts, limiting them to once or twice a week. Apples, bananas, carrots, cucumbers, grapes, lettuce and raisins are just some examples of favorite foods. Frozen corn and peas that have

Fresh vegetables should be provided once or twice a week.

been warmed to room temperature are also a welcome treat! Be sure to wash and dry all fruits and vegetables to remove harmful chemicals and possible pollutants. Mice will nibble at items, but will not consume the entire quantity. Thus, it is important to remove uneaten or wilted foodstuffs daily. Because mice like to hide their food, run your hand through the bedding to check closely.

GRAINS

Mice love grains. They also enjoy breads, rice and cereals, although these should not have excess sugar or salt. Crackers, dog biscuits, oatmeal and corn are other examples of snacks mice enjoy. Pet stores sell a variety of wheat-based treats. Give these supplements sparingly to avoid obesity. Day-old (hard but not moldy) bread is a yummy treat for mice, who will happily munch away.

MEATS AND PROTEINS

Some wild mice, such as the shrewmouse, eat mainly insects and other small animals while living on the forest floor. You may find that your pet mouse will be interested in protein as well as plant products. If you decide to give your mouse protein, make sure it is plainly cooked and not spiced with anything that may upset your mouse's stomach. In addition to meats, proteins are found in eggs, lentils and legumes, which mice enjoy greatly. Mealworms, grubs and crickets can be purchased at many pet shops that carry reptiles. These will also be gladly accepted in small quantities if you don't object to handling them!

FOOD IN YOUR KITCHEN

Some of what we eat is not good for us, much less a tiny mouse. Potato chips, snack crackers, soda, candy, chocolate, cookies, desserts and all the other goodies are not healthy for your mouse and should not be offered. Children need to understand that even though the little mouse would love a chip, a thick piece of carrot is a much better option. Table scraps that would fit in the categories of fresh vegetables and fruits, grains and seeds and meats are okay—such as lettuce leaves without dressing, unspiced meats and chicken, bread soaked in milk, baked potato (without salt or butter) and other healthy alternatives.

> **IS THAT YOUR FINGER OR A SNACK?**
>
> It's tempting to feed mice through the bars of the wire cages, but this teaches them to expect food every time you approach. If you have younger children in the home, the mice may bite them, thinking that their little fingers are treats. Take mice out of the cage to offer treats or place the gift in a special dish. Veggies, fruits, meats and grains are sure to please your mice much more than your finger will!

How Much Food and Water?

An adult mouse will eat and drink throughout the day. Water must always be available. Monitoring water intake is a good way to make sure your pet is healthy. You can purchase a pre-marked water bottle or mark one yourself. This allows you to regulate whether water consumption is increasing or decreasing, which can signal health problems.

Feed mice as directed on the label. Don't be concerned if your mouse does not eat what the box says, so

*Pizza? Your
mouse may
love it, but
you should
only give it
sparingly.*

long as she is eating on a regular basis and is not too fat or too thin.

KEEPING YOUR MOUSE TRIM

Mice enjoy foods that are not good for them. They adore such fatty foods as sunflower seeds, peanuts, cheese (of course!), cooked eggs and bacon. It's no surprise that in large quantities, these items are not good for your mouse. Obesity can be a problem for

caged pets. The best cure is plenty of exercise and a balanced diet. Provide the appropriate toys and equipment and limit the amount of treats. Never substitute treats for proper nutrition. Some people think an obese animal is "cute." But is it really "cute" when a normally active creature is reduced to sitting passively in a corner, unable to move because of the extra weight?

Mice make such good laboratory specimens because they are prone to the same diseases we are, such as cancer, heart disease and high cholesterol. By giving your pet an overabundance of fatty foods, you are mimicking similar tactics that these studies employ. Giving an animal a good life means helping her lead the healthiest and most active life possible. Fatty treats should be closely watched and given very infrequently. Don't confuse food with love.

chapter 7

Vacations
and Your
Mouse

Mice are great pets to keep at home, but what do you do when you go on vacation? The answer to this question depends on where you are going and how long you will be away. Your mouse will miss you when you're gone, but he may not be able to travel with you, depending on your mode of transportation. Plan ahead whenever possible.

Have Mouse, Will Travel

The most important thing to decide before traveling with a pet is whether the pet is healthy enough to travel. If you have any concerns about your pet's health, visit the veterinarian before you go.

If you'll be driving in a large car and there will be ample space, there is no reason to disassemble your mouse's usual cage. But if you'll be away for just a short period of time, the mouse will be fine in a smaller traveling cage. Keep food in the cage, but remove the water bottle to prevent spills from occurring. Keep a piece of fresh fruit in the cage instead. Fleshy fruits like apples and grapes contain a lot of water and will keep the mouse hydrated on the trip. Once you arrive at your destination, replenish the water supply as quickly as possible. You can protect your mouse from drafts by placing a towel over the cage. If the bedding is likely to spill, place the cage in a larger box. Attach a card to the cage with your name, address and telephone number so that you can be contacted if you and your pet are accidentally separated.

Traveling by Car

Traveling by car with your pet is perhaps the easiest mode of transportation. The mouse can be placed in a larger box on the floor of the car and protected from too much light and wind. Because you will be deciding how far you will be traveling and how often you'll be resting, you can accommodate your pet's needs.

Traveling by Airplane

Notify the airlines ahead of time if you plan to bring your mouse on the plane with you. When you make your reservations, notify the agent that you will be carrying on your pet mouse. Some airlines have restrictions, such as "Only one pet per every two rows." Other airlines do not allow certain kinds of pets, such as rodents. (Although we can't understand why!) Airline requirements usually demand that the cage fit under the seat. If you will be traveling to an international destination, inquire about special health requirements, such as quarantines. While traveling, your mouse should be in the pet carrier at all times. A crowded airport or airplane is the last place you would want to lose your pet.

Not only do airlines need to be called ahead, but the train and bus lines must be called as well. Some local carriers will allow you to transport your mouse if he is in his cage. Other lines may not be as willing to accommodate you. Greyhound, for example, has a "No pets, no exceptions" policy.

Leaving Your Mouse at Home
HOME ALONE

Mice can be left home alone if you will be away for a brief period of time (two or three days) and if sufficient food and water are provided. In these situations, it is imperative that water bottles be functioning properly to prevent dehydration. If possible, ask a friend to check on your mouse while you are away, if only to look in and make sure he has food and water.

FRIENDS AND FAMILY

Part of being a good mouse keeper is to discover ahead of time which friends are able to care for your pet if you are away. Not everyone appreciates a mouse. You may find that some of your friends who admire your mouse in your home become anxious at the thought of caring for him. Don't be upset if someone you consider a good friend declines your request. He or she may not feel comfortable with the responsibility. Family members, too, may also be uncomfortable. Look for someone who is enthusiastic about providing the care. This way, your pet is sure to receive attention as well as food and water.

> **A GUIDE FOR YOUR MOUSE SITTER**
>
> For friends, family or sitters who are willing to care for your pet mouse, provide a list of chores that need to be done while you are away. Be sure to write them down so that they are not forgotten. List the times when you feed and play with your mouse. Include your veterinarian's name, telephone number and address. Highlight any warnings that may be relevant, especially if your friend or family member has other pets or small children and has never cared for a mouse before. Leave some extra money in case the caretaker runs out of food or the mouse needs to go to the veterinarian. Be sure to leave your phone number should an emergency arise or the sitter has a question.

PET SITTERS

If friends and family are unavailable, look in the phone book for pet sitters. Many pet sitters are members of Pet Sitters International. This group can direct you to a pet sitter in your area when you dial (800) 268-SITS. Pet sitters will often look after your home by bringing in mail, watering plants and turning lights off and on so that the house appears occupied. Independent sitters may be costly, and you will want to find out more about the reliability of the individuals you are allowing into your home.

A responsible person should look after your mouse's needs while you're away.

Boarding Your Mouse

Most veterinarians will board your pet mouse. The benefit of boarding a mouse is that someone is not only available to check on your mouse, but will know what to do if the mouse takes ill. The cost of boarding your mouse at a clinic varies from place to place, but you may be able to negotiate a bit if you provide the cage, bedding and food. A clinic will usually have enough space to accommodate a mouse, but always investigate ahead of time.

chapter 8

Keeping Your
Mouse
Healthy

Mice are generally healthy animals, and of course it's best to start off with a healthy pet. You must learn to recognize the signs of a healthy mouse: Good appetite, glossy fur, bright eyes, an active nature and meticulous grooming habits.

Illness and injury in mice are generally due to improper nutrition, poor husbandry, unsafe handling and age. Preventing illness and injury are much simpler than treating these problems. I cannot over-emphasize the importance of the following tips—they'll go far to help your mouse lead a happy, healthy life.

Health Care Essentials

- **Cages must be properly maintained.** Good house-keeping is the best way to care for your friend. Keep cages clean and at moderate temperatures. Avoid drafty, damp spots and direct sunlight. Change bedding regularly. Scrub cages thoroughly, including corners and between the bars.

- **Provide a balanced diet and access to plenty of fresh water.** Wash fruits and vegetables before serving them to your mouse and promptly remove any uneaten products before they become wilted or moldy. Do not overfeed your little mouse.

- **Provide toys—an important part of any mouse's life.** They are useful in combating obesity and boredom.

- **Mice are susceptible to salmonella poisoning from raw meat and should never be given it.** Treat your pet to tiny amounts of cooked, unseasoned meats only once or twice a week.

- **Monitor what your pet eats and drinks and how often she eliminates.** By knowing your mouse's habits, you can better understand your pet. Isolate sick and aggressive animals.

- **When you're removing a sick mouse from a cage that houses other mice who appear healthy, dispose of all bedding and thoroughly disinfect the cage and all accessories.** When caring for an ill mouse, wash your hands before touching the other mice. This is the best way to help prevent the possible spread of disease. It is also wise to have an extra cage on hand in case animals become aggressive and injure one another.

- **It is imperative that mice are handled properly.** If a mouse accidentally falls or is sat on, this can kill the pet. Always treat your mouse as the fragile animal she is. Adults must supervise small children at all times. Instill in children the importance of playing gently and respecting these tiny animals.

- **Even with the best of care, you may need to bring your mouse to a veterinarian.** Choose a veterinarian before you need one. Not all veterinarians are experienced with mice and other small animals, and in an emergency, you'll want to know who to call. Even doctors, despite their best intentions, may have prejudices against these rodents that we cannot understand. A good veterinary clinic will be happy to answer any preliminary questions you may have, even before you acquire your mouse.

If you need to medicate your mouse, be sure to have your veterinarian advise you on the proper dosage and method.

- **If your mouse does have a health problem, be sure to follow your veterinarian's advice.** The doctor may be able to advise you over the phone or you may have to visit the clinic with your pet.

- **If possible, try to plan ahead for the unexpected expense a visit to the vet may bring, even if it may not be a costly trip.** This financial preparation allows you to make decisions at a potentially time-sensitive moment without having to choose between your economic situation and a much beloved pet. Always inform the veterinarian when you have more than one mouse so that necessary treatment can be applied to all animals.

Medicating Your Mouse

Because mice are so tiny, a little medicine goes a long way. Never give your mouse medication unless instructed to do so by the veterinarian. Some illnesses have similar symptoms but different causes. Unless a doctor diagnoses a particular problem and prescribes a specific medication, you run the risk of further injury to your mouse. It is imperative that you always follow the directions on the label of the medication. Never assume that "more is better" when giving a mouse medicine. For example, the products used in treating parasites are designed to kill living creatures (the mite or louse) and can have the same effect on your pet when dispensed in large quantities.

As mentioned above, follow your veterinarian's advice. Don't give medicine for human consumption to a mouse unless advised to do so by your veterinarian. Some medicines are fine for us, but toxic to your mouse. And never give medication prescribed for another animal without the veterinarian's approval.

> **USE MEDICATION WITH CAUTION**
>
> Use caution when giving your mouse medication. Always ask the veterinarian how much and how often to give the medication. Do not do any of the following unless directed to by a veterinarian:
>
> • Do not give your mouse medicine for humans.
>
> • Do not give your mouse medicine prescribed for another animal.
>
> • Do not give your mouse more medication than is prescribed.

Common Health Problems

There are a few health concerns that are seen with some frequency. These problems may be quite apparent, such as diarrhea or the loss of fur, or they can be a less obvious condition, such as lethargy or agitation. By interacting with your mouse every day, you're most likely to notice when she is under the weather.

BARBERING

Barbering is a condition usually seen in female mice. A dominant female will chew off the whiskers and the fur around the face and eyes of other females to assert her place as the lead mouse. It won't be difficult to distinguish the dominant female—she is the only one with any fur remaining. A possible solution is to separate the controlling female from the rest of the group. However, this might be a temporary solution as another female may assume her role. Male mice are more likely to bite and fight one another than engage in this behavior.

A variety of toys will help keep your mouse fit and prevent boredom.

BOREDOM

You may wonder about the significance of boredom to your pet's health, but don't underestimate this issue. A mouse who is isolated from physical contact with other animals will become bored. A bored mouse may react by rubbing or beating herself against the cage and throwing herself against objects within the cage. This repeated action is meant to soothe the mouse, in much the same way a dog might lick the same spot on her front leg or a human may chew his fingernails. Instead of actually relaxing the animal, the activity will cause injury. Constant rubbing causes the development of sores, which in turn may lead to infection.

To prevent such conditions, make sure your mouse has plenty of toys and personal contact, either with you or with another mouse. Mice in captivity are much less active than wild mice who are actively engaged in hunting for food, foraging for materials with which to build the nest and grooming members of the colony. Boredom can have serious effects on the captive mouse.

*Housing mice
together keeps
them happy and
stimulated.*

DEHYDRATION

Dehydration is a serious condition. Without any water, mice will die in as little as two days. Be sure to check the water bottle every day, making sure that the bottle is filled and that the stopper is not plugged. If a large amount of water is missing every day, it may be a sign that the bottle is leaking. Check for wet bedding. Mice may also push bedding into the spout and block the flow of water. Illness, particularly respiratory disorders and diarrhea, can also lead to dehydration. When a mouse doesn't feel well, she will not engage in routine behavior and can become dehydrated quickly. If you suspect illness, call your veterinarian immediately.

DENTAL PROBLEMS

It is not uncommon for a mouse to have problems with her teeth. Mice rely on their ability to gnaw to survive, so you must pay strict attention to their mouths. Broken teeth are usually the result of nutritional deficiencies. Consult your veterinarian for recommendations because your mouse cannot eat without her teeth.

Mice can also suffer from misaligned teeth, which cannot function properly. If the teeth are misaligned, a mouse may not be able to wear them down sufficiently through gnawing. When a mouse's incisors grow too long, they may pierce the skull and kill the mouse, or they may prevent the mouse from being able to eat at all and she will die of starvation. If you notice your mouse is having difficulty with her teeth, contact your veterinarian, who can clip the teeth. This solution is only temporary, however, and must be maintained as the teeth continue to grow.

DIARRHEA

Unformed, runny or smelly stools are not normal for mice and indicate a problem. As noted above, a mouse with diarrhea can become dehydrated. Access to water is mandatory. Whenever your mouse has such a condition, clean the cage immediately and as often as necessary. Be thorough.

Diarrhea may develop from a number of causes, such as improper diet; parasites such as tapeworms or roundworms; or poor cage hygiene, which can lead to the buildup of the bacteria that cause disease. Obviously, if you know your mouse has been eating food that would cause the loose stools, discontinue giving that food. If you suspect an internal parasite, contact your veterinarian. He can diagnose these parasites with a sample of your pet's stool. A fecal analysis will tell the vet if your mouse has worms, and he will prescribe treatment. The diarrhea may also be caused by enteritis, inflammation of the bowels, which can be the result of these same worms, diet and bacterial infections. Tyzzer's Disease is caused by the bacterium *Bacillus piliformis*. It is frequently fatal and causes loss of appetite and weight loss as well as diarrhea. If your veterinarian does not discover worms, he will probably examine your pet for one of these other problems.

HEATSTROKE

Mice are comfortable in a temperature around 68°F (20°C), which is usually considered average room temperature. A temperature close to or above 88°F (30°C) can cause heatstroke and death. Mice living in aquariums or other similar cages that sit directly in the sun run a great risk of heatstroke. Think of being in a sealed-up car on a hot summer's day. The temperature inside the cage rises to a level higher than that outside the cage. Because mice cannot sweat, they will groom themselves to cool down—but grooming is no cure-all and won't help animals if the temperature gets to high. If you find your mouse lying prone from heatstroke, there is usually not much you can do to help her. Use a washcloth to revive her with cool (not cold) water and call your veterinarian immediately. Sadly, a mouse is not likely to recover. Your best plan is to keep the cage away from direct sunlight.

INJURIES

Unfortunate occurrences are not uncommon with small creatures. If your mouse is accidentally dropped, sat on or injured in any way, call your veterinarian immediately. Internal injuries are as likely in a creature as small as a mouse as they are in a human. If you believe that your mouse has broken a bone, do not attempt to fix it yourself. Call the doctor, who will probably want to examine the animal. Any adjustments you attempt can cause further injury. If a male mouse is bleeding due to a fight, separate the fighters. Wounds from fighting can become infected. If you see an abscess forming (discussed below), be sure to contact your veterinarian.

SIGNS OF ILLNESS

Contact a veterinarian if you notice any of the following symptoms: weight loss, diarrhea, loss of appetite, ruffled fur, depression, lethargy, wheezing or funny breathing, chattering, dehydration, discharge from eyes or nose, bald spots, crusty skin, sores or repeated scratching. A mouse who is sick should be handled as little as possible.

PARASITES

Mites, lice and fleas are three active parasites that love to munch on mice. Although they are not commonly seen in isolated pets, mice can be exposed to these bugs by coming into contact with contaminated bedding or other materials brought in from the outdoors to serve as toys.

Although treatments for external parasites are available, they are not always easy to use. Before treating for parasites, bring your mouse to the veterinarian for an accurate diagnosis. The doctor will either provide you with the proper medication or tell you which one to purchase. Not all products are designed to be effective against all parasites so it is unwise to simply bring home a treatment from the pet supply store.

Mites are very small and are generally the most diffi-cult for the pet owner to see. The coat of an infected mouse may appear greasy with most fur missing behind the ears and the neck.

Lice are easier to see, and generally remain with a spe-cific mouse unless they come into direct contact with another potential host. Lice are relatively uncommon in mice.

Fleas are the most noticeable parasite—although you may not see their flattened brown bodies, you are likely to glimpse the flea feces. Looking a bit like coffee grinds, this flea debris turns right back into its original product when wetted: blood. Because fleas are more than happy to hop off the mouse and take a blood meal from the mouse's owner, treating your mouse means comfort to you and your pet.

Ringworm

Ringworm is not actually a worm, as the name implies, but is caused by a fungus. Bald patches appear with a raised, crusty ring in the center of the patch. Not only does the fungus spread easily from mouse to mouse, but it is highly communicable to other animals, includ-ing humans. Contact your veterinarian for treatment. Be sure to wash your hands thoroughly when handling a mouse that you believe has ringworm.

RESPIRATORY DISEASE

Respiratory disease is a serious condition. A cold can quickly turn into pneumonia and kill the mouse. Symptoms include lethargy, sneezing, heavy breathing or wheezing, chattering, dehydration, weight loss and discharge from the eyes or nose. Colds are usually due to contraction of a virus or exposure to bacteria, but may also be the result of sloppy housekeeping or exposure to changing temperatures. Respiratory infec-tions tend to arise suddenly, so keep a close watch for symptoms.

Do not handle your mouse too much; the stress caused by over-handling can have an adverse reaction at this critical time. Keeping the pet warm is a good first step. Your mouse should see a veterinarian as soon as possible, because respiratory disease advances quickly. Keeping the mouse away from drafts, proper feeding and maintenance and strict attention to your mouse's habits are good protection against respiratory illness.

A shiny, clean coat is a sign of good health.

Skin Disease

Skin problems are one of the easiest conditions to notice. Instead of having a clean and glossy coat, a mouse with skin problems will be in an obvious state of discomfort from the various symptoms. These symptoms include scratching, greasy or missing fur, hair loss, bald or patchy areas, crusty skin, sores and scabs. A mouse with skin disease may also suffer from depression, weight loss and a number of other problems.

Naturally, an itchy mouse will scratch. Such scratching can then lead to bald patches. Rubbing exposed skin causes sores and inflammation (dermatitis), leaving the skin susceptible to further wounds, which can lead to serious infections if not treated.

These problems of the coat and skin are generally caused by a reaction to food, deficiencies in the diet or parasites. In order to treat the problem, however, the cause must be properly diagnosed. Consult a veterinarian before beginning any treatment.

Food Allergies

A mouse may be allergic to something she ate. If you are certain your pet was not exposed to any parasites, you may suspect a food allergy. Some mice are known to react to certain kinds of formulated mixes. Because it can be difficult to determine the exact cause, limit your mouse's staple diet to food formulated specifically for mice. Supplement with basic vegetables, such as carrots. Do not give any other treats. The problem should dissipate in about two weeks. If there is an improvement, you have probably discovered the source of the scabs and itching.

Your veterinarian may recommend adding supplements to your mouse's food for a nutritional boost.

Diet Deficiencies

Just as it is important for humans to have all the proper vitamins, minerals and trace elements, it is equally important for the little mouse. If you're not giving your mouse a staple diet with proper supplements, but you have eliminated food allergies as the source of the problem, a deficiency in these dietary components may be to blame for the skin disease. A nutritionally complete diet is responsible for keeping the coat (as well as the rest of the mouse) healthy. Putting your mouse on the proper diet is the first step. If your mouse is on a healthy diet, make sure that the food is not stale, as nutrients are lost as food ages. If you suspect that your pet is not receiving all the nutrients she needs, ask your veterinarian about supplementing her meals with additives.

STRESS

Despite their hardy character and desire to live along-side man, mice can be easily stressed in a human-controlled environment. Different illnesses, such as respiratory infections, bite wounds and diarrhea, are outgrowths of stressful conditions. Overcrowding, over-handling and boredom are just a few examples of what causes stress.

Large ears provide a mouse with a very keen sense of hearing. To avoid undue stress, keep your mouse in a relatively quiet area of the home.

An easily overlooked source of stress in mice is noise. Mice normally communicate at high frequencies that we are unable to discern. Our ears hear frequencies of 3000 Hz, but the little mouse hears frequencies up to 100,000 Hz. Because their ears are more tuned to the noises in the environment, mice are more likely to hear sounds that do not bother us but disturb them greatly. We may hear a slight buzzing or squeaking from electronic equipment, but the sensitive mouse may hear a disturbing roar. If you have your mouse placed near any of these objects and notice she is anxious, move her to another location.

TUMORS AND ABSCESSES

Tumors are abnormal tissue growths or lumps that feel solid to the touch. They usually occur in older mice. Tumors in females are likely to develop in the mammary region; tumors in males are often located in the testes. Unfortunately, mice generally get malignant tumors, and so although veterinarians can surgically remove a tumor, the procedure does not often serve as a cure.

Tumors can be mistaken for an abscess, which is an area of pus surrounded by inflamed skin. An abscess is usually caused by bacteria and can appear around the eye or elsewhere on the body. Because the area needs to be drained and treated with antibiotics, contact your veterinarian if you notice any such condition. Abscesses are often seen in males that have been wounded while fighting. If you see your pets fighting, be sure to remove the aggressive male.

Wounds and Bites

A mouse may be injured by cutting herself on a sharp object or by a bite by another mouse. Such wounds can also develop into an abscess. It is possible for you to carefully bathe the wound in warm water, but call your veterinarian for possible treatments if the wound is infected. Bites usually occur when mice are forced to reside in overcrowded conditions. If you have multiple males, who are more likely to fight than females are, make sure there is plenty of space for the mice.

Visiting the Veterinarian

Never be embarrassed about calling your veterinarian, even if you feel responsible for an injury or consider your question to be silly. People who work at animal clinics hear all types of questions and see different kinds of cases every day. They want to help you help your animal, but can only do so if you call them and are honest about what you know. Their job is not to judge you, but to assist you in caring for your pet. In the case of an emergency, bring the pet in no matter what time of the day it is.

Bringing your mouse to the clinic can be stressful for her. Be sure to cover the cage with a blanket that allows air circulation, yet protects the mouse from drafts and exposure. This can also protect the mouse from other pets that are visiting the clinic. Some people do not take responsibility for their animals and allow their cats and dogs to walk around the clinic without a leash, so you will want to protect your mouse from these inquisitive predators. If you are transporting an injured mouse, you may want to carry her in a shoebox with a lot of padding. Use a towel or washcloth to cushion the mouse.

Making the Visit Fruitful

Try to bring your mouse to the veterinarian's office in her own cage. This allows the veterinarian to evaluate your pet in her normal living conditions and may provide valuable clues about any illness. If this option is not possible and you must bring the pet to the clinic in a traveling cage, be sure to tell the veterinarian about the pet's normal living conditions, complete with information on your cleaning and feeding habits and your mouse's typical routine. Be as specific as possible about your pet's medical history: How long has your mouse been ill? What specific symptoms have you seen? Have the symptoms gotten worse or improved? How old is your mouse? When and how did you acquire her? Did she eat anything unusual recently? Did she fall or jump from any place? Has she been in close contact with any other pets?

If children are the primary caregivers, parents should try to schedule the appointment when the children can be present—they can be quite knowledgeable about their own pet's health and very helpful to the veterinarian. If your animal is ill and you have other mice that are not present, be sure to notify the doctor in case treatment applies to all mice.

Mature Mice

An elderly mouse needs special care. Mice are considered adults at 6 weeks of age and "senior" as young as 1 year of age. As your mouse ages, she will be more easily affected by her surroundings, more susceptible to changes in temperature, drafts and direct light. You may also notice changes in her appearance, such as a hunched back, a decrease in appetite and activity, a dull coat, yellowing teeth or skin lesions. Speak with your veterinarian about such conditions, especially if you notice she is becoming too thin or she is less able to gnaw on things and her teeth aren't wearing down.

At an older age, mice will be less interested in meeting new people and being handled. Respect your elderly friend's needs and adapt your interaction to her changing abilities.

Euthanasia

If your pet is suffering, you may have to make a difficult decision. Euthanasia is commonly known as "putting the mouse to sleep" and involves an injection of anesthesia into the chest cavity. It is a difficult decision to make and one that must be based on the owner's insight into the quality of life an animal enjoys. If you see that your animal is in pain or age or sickness has limited the quality of your pet's life, your veterinarian can provide you with information about this option. Sometimes people try to hold onto their pets because it is so hard to say good-bye, but putting your little companion's needs first can also bring you peace of mind.

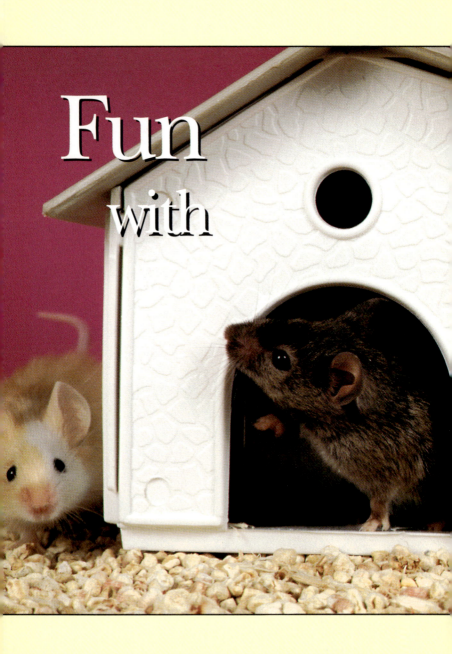

Fun
with

part three

Fancy Mice

chapter 9

Mouse
Varieties

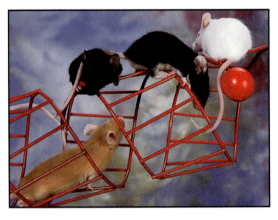

Mice are easy to recognize. The average mouse weighs less than 1 ounce (30 grams), has a thin tail, a sleek little body, slightly protruding eyes and round ears. When people think of pet mice, they usually think of the albino mouse. This mouse has no pigment and is characterized by a perfectly white coat and shiny pink eyes, pink feet and a pink tail. However, mice have a multitude of coat colors and types; these varieties are referred to as fancy mice.

"Fancy" means hobby or show mice. These mice are bred for exhibition. There are thousands of variations, and the number is growing as more colors, coat types and eye combinations are discovered. Most of these discoveries are the results of our fascination with diversity. As people bred mice for more unusual colors, the mouse fancy blossomed into a worldwide event.

The History of Fancy Mice

The exact date that humans began breeding mice for pets is difficult to determine. It is believed that people first trapped and kept Agouti mice. Agouti, or "wild-colored" mice, traditionally had a brown body marked with dark and light hairs that served to camouflage the wild creature. Written confirmation of white spotted mice present in China dates back to 1100 B.C. By selectively breeding albino mice with different types of mice, hobbyists obtained new varieties.

The Japanese are credited with being the original mouse fanciers and were early breeders of a variety of hues. European fascination with mice of different colors grew, particularly in the United Kingdom. Walter Maxey, an Englishman, was especially interested in breeding different colors of mice and in 1877 earned recognition as the "father of the fancy." He was one of the original founders of the National Mouse Club in 1895. This organization set standards for the varieties that are exhibited in shows.

> **WHAT ARE FANCY MICE?**
>
> The albino mouse, with a beautiful white coat and pink eyes, is not the only mouse around. Fancy mice are mice with different coat types, colors and markings. Their eyes can be pink or black. Colors can range from the purest white to the darkest black, with almost every color in between. Their coats can have short hair, long hair, frizzy hair, curly hair or no hair at all. Some mice have spots, others have bands. Coats can be glossy or they can be satiny with a super shine. Mice may come in many different varieties, but all can be great friends.

The American Mouse Fancy

Americans discovered fancy mice about seven decades later, founding the American Mouse Club in the 1950s. This organization is no longer in existence, but other groups of mouse fanciers have been created. These organizations including the Rat and Mouse Club of America; American Fancy Rat and Mouse Association; Mouse and Rat Breeders Association; American Rat, Mouse &

Hamster Society; Rat, Mouse and Hamster Fanciers, Midwest Rat and Mouse Club and Northeast Rat and Mouse Club International. These associations provide a forum for people to learn more about mice, to introduce a new coat type or color in mice, to come together to enjoy the variety of colors of mice and to share with others the excitement about their own little pet (the clubs are listed in the resources section, page 124).

Each club sets its own standards for acceptable coat types and colors, called varieties. These standards are the credentials by which most mice are recognized. The clubs may have similar standards, or they may choose not to recognize some varieties. Some fancy clubs may use different names to describe similar coat types. Other clubs may not recognize a mouse that has a certain eye color. Still another club may accept different colors or definitions of colors as standards. If you are interested in purchasing a special animal to show, become involved with a local club to get a greater understanding of the variety of mice and how judges define "star quality."

A longhaired mouse may be the perfect pet for you.

Coat Types

Mice have a variety of coat types that vary depending upon the individual hairs making up the coat. A standard coat consists of short hairs that lie flat against the body and have no wave. Longhair coats are silky and dense. These coats are grown out as long as possible, almost twice as long as the standard coat. Some of these mice look like they need a haircut! Mice with frizzy coats have curls or waves all over the body. The frizzy coat can be short-haired or longhaired. Frizzy longhairs may resemble a little powder puff! Mice can have a combination of these coat styles, or they may have no coat at all and be hairless. Keep in mind that not every organization recognizes all the varieties, and some fancy clubs may use different names to describe the coat types.

Self mice are available in a variety of colors, including cream.

Colors

Coat colors vary even more than coat types. Mice may have one or more colors. Their coats may have obvious spots, just little flecks of color or the color may be broken by large patches of white. The varieties of colors are referred to as solid (self), ticked, shaded and marked. As with coat type, not all colors are recognized by the fancy clubs. If the colors are recognized, they may be classified in different groups.

SELF MICE

The word "self" describes mice of a single, solid color. The uniform color covers the body with no other markings or shadings present. Self mice come in a wide range of colors including beige, black, blue, champagne, chocolate, coffee, cream, dove, fawn, gold, ivory, lilac, orange, red, silver and white. The self white mouse may have pink or black eyes, but is not the same as an albino mouse with his ruby eyes.

Tan and Fox

Tan and fox mice have similar coats, so they are often grouped together. A tan mouse has a solid-colored topcoat and a tan belly. A fox mouse also has a solid topcoat, but has a white belly. There is clear definition between the two colors.

Note the light-colored belly on this tan mouse.

Ticked

Ticked coats have a solid base coat with other colors "ticked" through it, creating the illusion of a uniform color. This classification usually includes the following varieties:

Agouti As a color of "wild" mice, agouti was traditionally a dark brown blended with black and yellow hairs, but breeding the mouse cultivated a light brown. The coat is ticked with black hair as well, and the belly may be a silver color.

Argente The blue base coat of this color is ticked with light fawn. The mouse has a lighter belly.

Chinchilla Resembling the coat of the chinchilla, this base coat is a light gray ticked with brown or black hairs. The mouse has a white belly.

Cinnamon The cinnamon mouse strongly resembles the agouti, and they are often confused. But the cinnamon coat is a lighter color, a golden-brown ticked with a darker brown as opposed to the agouti black.

Marked Marked mice usually have white spots or markings that cover a darker base coat. This classification usually includes the following varieties:

Dutch—This mouse looks just like the Dutch rabbit. Color covers the face in two patches. These patches are separated by a blaze, or white area, that travels up the center of the face. The mouse's midsection is a pure white until the rump, which is a solid color.

Broken and Even—These two color variations are grouped together by some clubs. The coloration is also referred to as white spotted or pied, which is defined as blotches of two or more colors. These mice have a white base coat with colored spots and patches that are precisely shaped. Uniform placement is considered an even color, whereas irregular arrangements are defined as broken.

Variegated—This coloration is nearly identical to the broken and even colors. Unlike the clear-cut markings of the broken or even colors, however, this coat has imperfect color splashed across the white base coat.

Belted or Banded—The colored mouse is encircled by a band of white that can vary in size and location.

The chinchilla variety's coat is a pale gray ticked with darker hairs.

Rumpwhite—In this color type, the legs, tail and rear one-third of the mouse's body is white, and the rest of the body is colored.

Silvered   The base coat of this color can be black, blue or brown, ticked with white or off-white hairs, giving the mouse a silvery look.

Shaded   Shaded mice have two distinct colors. The body color is offset by another color, highlighting points on the body (ears, nose, feet, tail). The two more common colors are Himalayan and Siamese. The Himalayan mouse looks like a Himalayan rabbit, with a white or off-white body and any recognized color covering the points. A Siamese mouse has the coloring of a Siamese cat. This color is also known as seal-point Siamese. Other colors include blue-point Siamese (a blue version) and reverse Siamese (an inversion of the seal-point coloring).

111

Other Varieties

REX

The frizzy mouse is classified as the Rex in some clubs. They can be referred to as frizzy or fuzzy, depending upon how tightly the hair curls. Rex mice coats are seen in a variety of colors. Whiskers are curly or bent.

A cinnamon mouse relaxes in his owner's hand.

SATIN

A radiant shine is the hallmark of this coat type. The soft, short coat and the extra-shiny finish magnify the coat color, giving it a vivid look. Mice can be frizzy or longhaired, tan or fox or a multitude of colors.

ENGLISH MICE

English mice are fancy mice imported from England or purebred descendants of such mice. These mice are from a fancy that is almost 100 years older than the American fancy. As a result, English mice are more tame and have well-defined features. Traditionally, this mouse is larger and has a longer tail, larger ears and a more streamlined body than his American cousin. Americans have started breeding American fancy mice with English mice to improve the quality of their American mice. When an English mouse and an American mouse are placed next to one another, the difference is quite clear. It is difficult to find English mice in American pet stores, so attend a mouse show if you are interested in seeing them.

A broken coat is characterized by irregular spots of color on a white base.

HAIRLESS, BALD OR NAKED MICE

Hairless mice, also referred to as bald or naked mice, are standard in some fancy organizations. They resemble newborn mice and are bald with translucent skin that is usually pink. They may have short whiskers or no whiskers at all. Sometimes their skin is wrinkled. These mice can be susceptible to scratches and injuries because they lack the extra protection a coat provides. Hairless mice are especially sensitive to hot and cold temperatures. Some people object to breeding hairless mice because their baldness is originally the result of a hereditary disease and breeding the mouse continues the genetic mutation. Others find delight in these mice.

WALTZING MICE

Waltzing mice, known also as dancing mice, are not mice blessed with the gifts of Fred Astaire or Ginger Rogers, but are mice suffering from a genetic disorder. Waltzing mice have a flaw in the inner ear that destroys their sense of balance. Waltzing mice are unable to walk in a straight line and instead walk in circles. The mouse is usually Dutch marked (black and white) and deaf. Compared to the average mouse, waltzing mice are smaller and have a shorter life span. Some people will try to sell this poor mouse as a "normal" mouse with a special talent. Be aware of the true nature of this disorder and of the type of person who would sell an animal like this for profit.

SINGING MICE

The grasshopper mouse, so named for his taste for grasshoppers and other insects, loves to sing in the Mexican desert air. Standing on hind legs with his head thrown back, this mouse will make a series of high-pitched cries. Some people report that their domesticated mouse has the same ability. However, scientists have studied such mice and concluded that this is not the same behavior. The "singing" of the domesticated mouse is actually a disorder in the nose and throat that makes the mouse's breathing sound as if he has musical talent.

PURCHASING A MOUSE FOR SHOW

If you've decided that you would like to show your mouse and that you would like a fancy mouse, you can meet breeders at shows or locate them by contacting a mouse club. When buying from a breeder, apply the same scrutiny to your new pet as you would if you were shopping at a store. You will want a mouse with no flaws that prevent the animal from competing. As with any purchase, feel free to ask questions without being pressured to purchase the mouse. The more mice you look at and the more reading you do about different club standards, the easier it will be for you to discern which is the right mouse for you.

Exotic Mice

Along with derivations of the common house mouse, "exotic" mice have become popular pets as well. These animals have the same needs as common pet mice, such as a proper cage and nest box, bedding, food, water and toys. Exotic pets often require more time to be tamed because they are closer to their wild relatives than the domesticated house mouse. Some exotics never take to being held.

Another disadvantage to owning an exotic pet is that there is sometimes little information—and even fewer veterinarians—available to owners of these less common pets. The information below is only a brief introduction to exotic mice. If you are interested in acquiring these delightful pets, be sure to do more research before purchasing them. The Internet and pet magazines offer some basic information that describes the needs of these exotic pets. The more you know about the responsibility of these enchanting critters, the easier it will be for you to decide if an exotic mouse is right for you. (See Chapter 11, "Recommended Reading and Resources," for more information.)

THE AFRICAN PYGMY MOUSE

The African pygmy mouse has caught people's attention with his tiny size. A full grown mouse measures less than 3 inches, including tail, and weighs a mere 10 grams (¼ ounce)! This small creature is just as active as a domestic mouse, however, and loves to tunnel through different materials. In the wild, they prefer to eat seeds rather than plants, and the African pygmy mouse will munch on insects when they are available. Although albino mutations have been reported, the

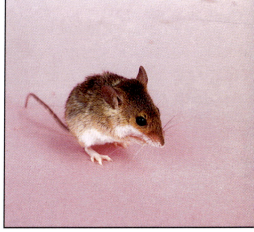

pygmy mouse is generally found in only one color. The cinnamon-colored coat and creamy white belly make the African pygmy mouse an attractive creature. Because they move quickly, pygmy mice can be difficult to capture and handle.

Take extreme care handling a tiny African pygmy mouse.

THE EGYPTIAN SPINY MOUSE

The Egyptian spiny mouse is named for the rough fur that covers his back. The honey-colored coat is sprinkled with darker fur on top that has a sharp feel. This coat varies in color from agouti to light cream and camouflages the mouse in the wild. Owners have been attracted to the spiny mouse's easy temperament and love of climbing. The Egyptian spiny mouse is a very active animal with a real affection for chewing; he will gnaw his way through almost anything.

"Spinies," as they are called by some breeders, differ from house mice in a number of ways. They're larger than the average domesticated house mouse and allegedly give off less odor than other mice. Gestation can last over forty days, which is a long time for mice.

Extra time in the womb allows babies to be born with their eyes open and covered with fur, unlike the babies of most rodents.

Spiny mice are the only mice to give birth standing up on all fours when they deli-

An Egyptian spiny's fur will feel rougher than that of other mice.

ver, assisted by other mice who gnaw at the embryonic membrane surrounding the newborns. The mother just has to hope that these "nurses" do not run off with her babies and try to claim them as their own!

THE ZEBRA MOUSE (OR AFRICAN STRIPED GRASS MOUSE)

The zebra mouse has exceptional markings—a continuous pattern of alternating light and dark brown stripes run from head to tail. The tail is quite long and dark, highlighted by a black stripe that begins at the back of the neck and extends over the tail. The zebra mouse is large, about the size of a small gerbil. Short whiskers and round ears accentuate the delicate features. This mouse is known for his speed, agility and desire to burrow, but is also considered a good companion in captivity. In the wild they are quite timid, dashing about during the day, eating grasses, grains and insects. When babies are born, they have a thin coat and the stripes are already visible.

THE DORMOUSE (NOT REALLY A MOUSE AT ALL!)

The dormouse, which is also becoming popular as an exotic pet, is not really a mouse at all. Mice and dormice belong to the same order (*Rodentia*), but they are grouped into different suborders. Mice belong to the suborder *Myomorpha,* or mouselike rodents. Dormice belong to *Glirimorpha,* or dormouse-group rodents.

Dormice resemble squirrels with their little bodies and bushy tails. Two dormice commonly kept as pets are the smaller African dormouse (*Graphiurus murinus*) and the larger edible (or fat) dormouse (*Glis glis*). Both species originated in Africa and resemble one another.

The zebra mouse is known both for its athleticism and its unusual markings.

The smaller dormouse has gray fur, is about 4 inches long and lives well in captivity. They are excellent climbers, moving about even on slick surfaces. In the wild they are active mostly at night, eating grains, seeds and insects, as well as small birds and their eggs.

The edible dormouse is so named because he is not only a pet, but also a delicacy. This dormouse is able to store a large amount of fat, which makes him a tasty meal. Ancient Romans raised this dormouse for food, and the animal is still eaten in Europe today. Fortunately for the dormouse, he is also gaining popularity as a pet. He can grow up to 8 inches long, including the tail, and is covered with thick, soft grayish-brown fur. Both types of dormouse will hibernate in cool weather.

117

chapter 10

Showing
Your
Mouse

Mouse shows are not as uncommon as you might think. Shows are held all over the country, as well as all over the world! People will show their mice for a variety of reasons. Some people enjoy meeting other pet lovers and sharing their knowledge. Many people want to exhibit mice that they've bred. Others just want the opportunity to show off a special pet.

To Show or Not to Show

Requirements and standards for showing your mouse will vary depending on where you live and which organization is hosting the show. To enter your mouse or to learn more about attending a show, contact an organization in your area. A number of them are listed in Chapter 11, "Recommended Reading and Resources." Consider attending some shows to learn what the judges look for and what will be required of you and your pet, both in time and preparation. Some clubs have guidelines regarding the age of mice in competition, while others have classes for mice of all ages.

Once you've decided to enter your mouse, obtain a schedule (you may have to pay a fee). If you're a member of a club, schedules will usually be mailed to you as a matter of course. You can also check your local newspapers and trade magazines for upcoming shows. The schedule contains information about classes your mouse can compete in and lists the rules of the show.

The club or organization will define the standards for their show; standards may differ from show to show. A standard mouse must have the approved coat, markings and body shape. It is important that you enter your mouse properly or she will be disqualified. If you're unsure about the proper class for your pet, club staff members will usually advise you. Be sure to register before the deadline.

> **MOUSE SHOW ETIQUETTE**
>
> Always ask permission to touch other people's mice. If someone would like to touch your mouse, it's perfectly okay to politely decline the request. Disinfect your hands before and after touching other mice to avoid spreading disease. Don't remove a mouse from the table without asking the judges during the judging. Have fun and bring money to buy more mice!

Preparing for the Show

Before the day of the show, complete all necessary forms and have all of your materials assembled. If you have questions, don't worry—they will be answered at registration. When showing any pet, keeping your stars clean and healthy is the first step to success. Look your mouse over before the show date to make sure she is healthy enough to travel and compete. There is not much more to preparing a mouse for show. Because most shows require a certain type of display cage and bedding for judging, contact the organization to find out its requirements if they aren't listed in the standards. Obviously, the cage and bedding should be immaculate. If you cannot find the right type of cage in your area, ask about renting a cage that day. Prepare enough bedding so that your mouse doesn't become cold at the show and hide. Mice are judged on temperament as well as appearance.

The Big Day

On the day of the show, give yourself plenty of time to set up and to have any questions answered. If you're not in a rush, you'll have a chance to meet other people and enjoy yourself. When you register, you can verify the class or classes your mouse should compete in. Clubs usually mandate a health check to ensure that all animals are healthy enough to compete. This helps to prevent disease from traveling among the animals at the show. Because some diseases lie dormant at first, an unsuspecting owner may bring an ill animal. It is always wise to use a disinfectant if you will be touching any mouse other than your own. Use this both before and after you come into contact with the other mice.

You'll find lots of different varieties of mice at a show.

Once your mouse has been approved for show, you may want to prepare your mouse and cage for the judges if judging begins soon. You may also have to wait if the rats or hamsters are judged before the mice. This is a good opportunity to see the competition and to discover interesting coat colors and variations.

With all the sweet mice and interesting people that come to a show, it is easy to become distracted. Be sure you don't miss the announcement that it's time to show your pet. Once you set your mouse on the judging table, you may not handle or touch the mouse again until the judging is complete and all judging has ended. As the judging continues you can learn a great deal about how the mice are judged and the qualities of a winner. Most judges are more than happy to speak with you at the end of the show if you are interested in learning more.

Showing Pet Quality Mice

Mice don't need to be of the fancy variety to compete in shows. Although highly-bred mice are more likely to win, a good quality pet purchased from a pet shop still has the opportunity to compete. These mice are considered "unstandardized" mice, or mice that do not fit into recognized categories. Some organizations offer shows that are strictly for pets. This is an opportunity for everyone to have a good time. The show rules are generally the same irrespective of the mice being shown, but classes are more informal and organized for everyone's enjoyment.

part four

Beyond the Basics

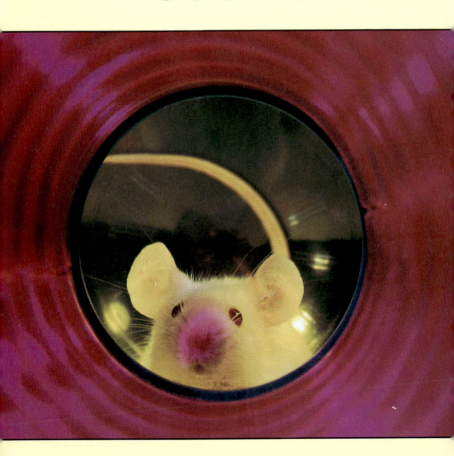

chapter 11

Recommended Reading and Resources

There are many magazines, clubs, and Internet opportunities for mice enthusiasts. New books and magazines emerge all the time. As with anything you see in print, use it as a guide. If you find something that may apply to your pet, but you are unsure, check with your veterinarian.

Internet

The Internet offers a wealth of information, but sites are continuously changing. Try searching the words "mouse" or "fancy mouse" or "rodent."

Books

Bielfeld, Horst. *Mice: A Complete Pet Owner's Manual.* Hauppauge, NY: Barron's Educational Series, Inc., 1985.

Hirschhorn, Howard. *Guide to Owning a Mouse.* Neptune, NJ: TFH Publications, Inc., 1996.

Sife, Wallace, Ph.D. *The Loss of a Pet, 2nd Ed.* New York: Howell Book House, 1998.

Siino, Besty Sikora. *You Want What for a Pet?!* New York: Howell Book House, 1996.

Taylor, David. *Small Pet Handbook.* Hauppauge, NY: Barron's Educational Series, Inc., 1997.

Magazines

Rat & Mouse Gazette
55 Valley View Dr.
Fitchburg, MA 01420-2138
www.rmca.org/Gazette

Critters USA
Fancy Publications
P.O. Box 6050
Mission Viejo, CA 92690
www.animalnetwork.com/Critters

Clubs

Below is a list of clubs that hold meetings and shows. Most have Internet sites that will allow you to connect with them or with sister clubs that do not appear on the list below. They may also have information on how to start a club in your area if you are unable to locate a club close to you!

American Fancy Rat and Mouse Association (AFRMA)
9230 64th St.
Riverside, CA 92509
www.afrma.org

American Rat, Mouse & Hamster Society (ARMHS)
P.O. Box 1451
Ramona, CA 92065

Mouse & Rat Breeders Association
127 Stockbridge Lane
Ojai, CA 93023

North American Rat and Mouse Club International (NRMCI)
603 Brandt Ave.
New Cumberland, PA 17070
www.geocities.com/Heartland/Ranch/3220

**Rat and Mouse Club of America (RMCA)—Home
Chapter**
13075 Springdale St. # 302
Westminster, CA 92683
www.rmca.org

**Rat and Mouse Club of America (RMCA)—Colorado
Chapter**
P.O. Box 62655
Colorado Springs, CO 80962

Bay Area Rat and Mouse Club of America (BARMCA)
www.rmca.org/barmca

**Rat and Mouse Club of America—Southern
California Chapter**
13075 Springdale St.
Suite 505
Westminster, CA 92683
www.rmca.org/clubinfo/socal

Rat, Mouse and Hamster Fanciers (RMHF)
Animal World (membership)
198 School St.
Danville, CA 94526
www.ratmousehamster.com/rmhf

INTERNATIONAL

National Mouse Club of England
29 Manor Close
Tunstead, Norwich
Norfolk NR12 8EP
England

Australian National Rodent Association
P.O. Box 2079
Too wong
Brisbane, Queensland—Australia
http://members.tr.pud.com/anraq

Other organizations exist around the world and can be
located on the Internet.